ALEXIS ZEGERMAN

Alexis became Pearson Writer-in-Residence at Hampstead
Theatre, London, in 2007, where she is also under commission.
She joined the Royal Court Young Writers' Programme in 2001.
Her play *Killing Brando* received a public reading at the Young
Vic as part of Paines Plough's Wild Lunch in 2004, and was
later produced at Òran Mór in Glasgow for their 'A Play, a Pie
and a Pint' season. Short plays include *I Ran the World* for the
Royal Court/Flight 5065, and *Noise* at Soho Theatre, London
(winner of the Westminster Prize for New Playwriting 2003).
Her plays for BBC Radio 4 include *Ronnie Gecko* (Richard
Imison Award nomination), *Are You Sure?*, *The Singing Butler*,
Jump and *Déjà Vu* (a joint production with ARTE, France), and
the comedy series *School Runs*. Alexis is also an actress,
working both on stage and screen.

Alexis Zegerman

LUCKY SEVEN

NICK HERN BOOKS
London
www.nickhernbooks.co.uk

A Nick Hern Book

Lucky Seven first published in Great Britain as a paperback original in 2008 by Nick Hern Books Limited, 14 Larden Road, London W3 7ST

Lucky Seven copyright © 2008 Alexis Zegerman

Alexis Zegerman has asserted her right to be identified as the author of this work

Cover image: Eureka! (www.eureka.co.uk)
Cover design: Ned Hoste, 2H

Typeset by Nick Hern Books, London
Printed and bound in Great Britain by CPI Antony Rowe, Chippenham, Wiltshire

A CIP catalogue record for this book is available from the British Library

ISBN   978 1 85459 524 9

The Up Series

First broadcast in 1964, *7 Up!* was a groundbreaking documentary, made by Granada Television, which took fourteen British children from varied backgrounds, and encouraged them to talk about their lives, their aspirations and their hopes for the future.

It was the director Michael Apted who found the participants – ten boys and four girls – and it was he who saw the potential for a follow-up film. *7 Plus Seven* was broadcast in December 1970, *21 Up* seven years after that and so on, until *49 Up* in 2005. The series has proved hugely popular in both the UK and abroad, and the sequence is set to continue: *56 Up* is already planned. Because *7 Up!* was not intended to be the first of a series, no contracts were signed to include future programmes, and so all subsequent interviews have been voluntary. Some participants have dropped out through the years. Some have even returned after fourteen-year gaps. But all the subjects have turned out to be remarkably articulate, and watching them go through marriage and divorce, parenthood, success and disappointment in their careers has made for compelling television.

Lucky Seven is inspired by the *7 Up!* series, but all characters and situations are entirely fictional.

I would like to thank the following: Tony, Frances, Neil and everyone at Hampstead Theatre. The Pearson Playwrights' Scheme for their support with writing this play. Simon, Ola and Nina at the Royal Court Young Writers' Programme. Lucy, John and Vicky, formerly at Paines Plough. My friends and family for their belief, kindness and sense of humour.

Alexis Zegerman

Lucky Seven was first performed at Hampstead Theatre, London, on 5 November 2008 (previews from 31 October), with the following cast:

ALAN   David Kennedy
TOM   Jonny Weir
CATHERINE   Susannah Harker

Director   Anthony Clark
Designer   Liz Ascroft
Lighting Designer   Arnim Friess
Sound Designer   Gregory Clarke

For my mother

Characters

ALAN
TOM
CATHERINE

DAVID, *a recorded voice*

The actors playing Alan, Tom and Catherine play themselves from forty-nine to seven years old.

Setting

The stage is quite bare apart from a large three-seater sofa in the centre. At the back of the stage is a huge TV screen, which also doubles as a window offering a view across the city – London.

This text went to press before the end of rehearsals and so may differ slightly from the play as performed.

ACT ONE

(49)

Black.

A large '49' appears on the TV screen. Then disappears.

Lights up. The screen is now a giant window overlooking the current London skyline. Faint sound of cheering on the street below.

TOM (*49*) *sits on the sofa.* TOM *is thin, pale, good-looking. He wears a bright jumper, trousers and sensible shoes. His hair is gelled and styled to be ever-so-slightly trendy.* ALAN (*49*) *stands looking out the window.* ALAN *is stocky – overweight – and wears a suit. He looks unsettled.*

ALAN. What car did they give you?

TOM. Sorry?

ALAN. To bring you here. What car?

    TOM *thinks.*

TOM. I don't know.

ALAN. What type?

TOM. You always ask me this, Alan. I don't take any notice.

ALAN. What did it say on the boot?

TOM. I went round the front.

ALAN. Okay then. On the bonnet. Was there a winged angel? A three-pointed star thing – ?

TOM. A cat.

ALAN. A cat?

TOM. Yes. Well, more of a leopard.

ALAN. You mean a Jaguar.

TOM. It's hard to tell without the spot pattern.

ALAN. They brought you over here in a Jag?

TOM. Possibly.

ALAN. *Honda Accord*. Can you believe that? They brought me over here in a Honda Accord. That's not a car. It's a motorised sushi box. The Japanese can't do cars. They do small things for small people. Sushi. Tamagotchi –

TOM. Tsunami.

ALAN. Exactly. Last time they sent me a Mercedes. Tinted windows. Legroom. Now, say what you like about the Germans, they know how to make a car.

No wonder my knee's playing up.

Old sports injury.

TOM (*sighs*). Golf.

ALAN. Tough game. You don't play.

TOM. Actually, I do.

ALAN. Not for the faint – (*He stops*.) Do you?

TOM. Yes.

ALAN. Since when?

TOM. A few years ago.

ALAN. Oh. Right. What's your handicap? Besides the obvious.

TOM. I don't know. I play for fun.

ALAN. *Fun?*

TOM. I joined a club.

ALAN. You belong to a club?

TOM. Yes.

ALAN. *You* belong to a club?

TOM. Yes.

Beat.

ALAN. Where the hell's David?

TOM. On his way.

ALAN. He's definitely coming?

TOM. Of course he's coming.

ALAN. Yeah. He'll be in a proper car. One of those Holly-wood, chauffeur-driven, prick-mobiles. With bulletproof windows. And a fridge. Not a Honda Accord. Suspension like a bloody rickshaw. Might as well have hopped all the way down the A13.

ALAN limps over to the sofa.

Shove over.

TOM moves over so he's sitting in the middle. ALAN sits to his right.

Still don't have a motor?

TOM. No.

ALAN. Good. Congestion charge – it's a killer. Ruined small businesses. Not me, of course. I don't pay it. I've got a dis-abled badge.

TOM. Because of your knee?

ALAN. It's my mum's.

TOM. Your mother's dead.

ALAN. I know. Eight years. Bless her. I think of her every time I park the car.

Did you hear about Princess?

TOM. Her name's Catherine.

ALAN. All over the papers. Bloody journalists. Like vultures.

TOM. I read about it.

ALAN. Magpies stealing lives. They can't just leave you alone.

TOM. It got a lot of coverage.

ALAN. Yeah. She looked terrible in the photos. Older. Well, you would, wouldn't ya. Tragedy. It does that. Makes you think. Life. One moment. Then. You know.

It's all about luck.

TOM. I didn't think she'd be coming.

ALAN. David must have convinced her. He's very convincing.

TOM. I wanted to get in touch, but –

ALAN. We're not allowed.

TOM. No.

TOM *pulls out a card.*

I brought her a card.

ALAN. A sympathy card?

TOM. Sort of. Yes.

ALAN. Can I sign it?

TOM. No.

ALAN. Go on.

TOM. It's sealed.

ALAN. Unseal it.

TOM. No.

ALAN. Come on. Don't be selfish.

TOM. Get her your own card.

ALAN. I didn't have time.

TOM. We've had *years*.

ALAN. Forget it. I don't need a card. I'll give her my words. My heartfelt words. Not a card with flowers on it and a crappy poem.

I can open envelopes without anyone –

TOM. No!

Beat.

ALAN. Give us a hug.

TOM. Sorry?

ALAN. A hug. Come on. Seven years.

ALAN opens his arms out, and hugs a reluctant TOM. ALAN holds TOM, a bit too long for comfort. TOM eventually breaks away.

You put on a bit of weight.

TOM. Have I?

ALAN. On your face.

I've still got a few to lose.

TOM. Stones?

ALAN. Pounds. Came off those faddy diets. I just eat a little bit of what I fancy – like French women.

Don't get me wrong. You look good on it. Healthier. Have you started eating meat?

TOM. I've never been a vegetarian.

ALAN. Well, anyway, you look different.

TOM. I'm happy.

ALAN. What?

TOM. I said, I'm happy.

ALAN *laughs*.

ALAN. Nah.

TOM. Yes.

ALAN. You're not happy.

TOM. I am.

ALAN. *Misery guts?*

ALAN *stops laughing. Beat.*

Well, good for you. Seriously. Good for you. Where the
hell's David?

Keeping us waiting. I mean, who's running this bloody
circus?

ALAN *is nervy. He goes over to the window. There's some
cheering from a crowd outside. He moves away quickly.*

TOM. Are you all right?

ALAN (*laughs*). Am I all right? Well, this is a turn-up for the
books. You're asking me if I'm all right?

TOM. Yes.

ALAN. Oh. I'm fine. I'm peachy. I mean, I'm *busy*. I don't
need to be doing this, you know. This thing's run its course
for me. I'm only really here for David. *Herr Direktor*.
Steven bloody Spielberg. He calls up, doesn't he. As he
always does. Schmoozing. Saying how important I am to
the programme. The *most* important. Or loved. He might
have said *loved*. Anyway, the programme means a lot to
him. So… here I am.

ALAN *stops and looks out front.*

TOM. Alan, are you sure you're okay?

ALAN. Shhh. I think we're being watched.

TOM *looks out front*.

That camera's on.

TOM. I don't think it is.

ALAN. Listen.

They listen. TOM *shakes his head*.

Are you deaf? There's a noise. A whirring. We're being filmed.

TOM. It's possible.

ALAN. He can't do that.

TOM. Well, he can.

ALAN. Not with us unaware. It's not on. (*Suddenly.*) There it is again. The noise.

ALAN *gets down on his hands and knees, and looks under the sofa*.

TOM. What are you doing?

ALAN. Hidden cameras. Bugs. I can feel them crawling all over us. It's like an itch.

TOM. Would you like some water?

ALAN. No.

TOM. Is this about the car? Speak to David. I'm sure he'll get you a better car.

ALAN. I don't give a fuck about the car.

TOM. A Mercedes. Or a Leopard.

ALAN. *Jaguar*.

TOM. I'm sure it was just a mistake, Alan.

ALAN. This isn't a mistake. That jumper is a mistake. This is a *disaster*. This is a car crash with fatalities. This is being stuck on the M25. With no turn-off in sight. And going round and round for all eternity!

He stops. TOM *looks down at his jumper.*

Black.

(42)

A large '42' appears on the TV screen. Then disappears.

Lights up. The screen is now a giant window overlooking the London skyline befitting 2001.

TOM *(42) sits on the sofa.* TOM *is thin, pale, good-looking. He wears a plain jumper, trousers and sensible shoes. His hair is gelled down into a conservative side-parting. He's holding a large brown envelope containing a manuscript.* ALAN *(42) stands looking out the window.* ALAN *is stocky – overweight – and wears a suit. He is much calmer than before.*

ALAN. What car did they give you?

TOM. Sorry?

ALAN. To bring you here. What car?

TOM *thinks.*

TOM. I don't know.

ALAN. What type?

TOM. I don't –

ALAN. Executive?

TOM. I'm not sure.

ALAN. Mercedes S-Class. Leather seats. Magazines in the back. Personally, I prefer a Bentley. Or a Jag. More legroom. I have to keep the weight off my knee.

I've got a sports injury.

Golf.

Do you play?

TOM. No.

ALAN. Not for the faint-hearted. Sand gave way in a bunker. Twisted my left knee.

I belong to a club. Very exclusive membership.

TOM. 'I wouldn't belong to a club that had me as a member.'

ALAN. Well, I wouldn't belong to a club that had you as a member.

TOM. No. *Me* as a member.

ALAN. That's what I said.

ALAN *limps to the sofa*.

Shove over.

TOM *moves*. ALAN *sits, as before*.

TOM. Do you think David's coming?

ALAN. Of course he's coming. Why wouldn't he come.

What you driving at the moment?

TOM. I don't.

ALAN. You don't?

TOM. No.

ALAN. Not at all?

TOM. It's irresponsible to have cars in metropolitan areas.

ALAN. I live in the country. I work in the city. I need a car.

TOM. You don't live in the country.

ALAN. I moved. More space. Fresh air. Indoor pool.

TOM. Where?

ALAN. Bushey.

    So how do you get to work then?

TOM. I cycle.

ALAN. Cycling's dangerous. I nearly knocked over a cyclist
    yesterday. You should be careful.

    Still a librarian?

TOM. Archivist.

ALAN. Right. At the newspaper library.

TOM. Archive.

ALAN. Keeps you out of trouble.

TOM. Yes.

    Beat.

ALAN. Seven years. Can you believe it?

    Come here –

TOM. Why?

ALAN. Give us a hug.

TOM. Sorry?

ALAN. Come on. Stand up and give us a hug.

TOM. I don't want to, Alan.

ALAN. We haven't seen each other for seven years.

    TOM *reluctantly gets up and gives* ALAN *a hug.* ALAN
    keeps hold of TOM *a bit too long for comfort.*

    You eating properly?

TOM. Yes.

ALAN. Lentils and buckwheat?

TOM. What if he doesn't come?

ALAN. David? Of course he's coming. He's the director.

TOM. Maybe he's too busy.

ALAN. This is his baby. *We're* his babies.

TOM. What if he's losing interest?

ALAN. You don't lose interest in your babies. You look after them. You nurture and feed 'em and watch 'em grow.

TOM. He's going to Hollywood.

ALAN. I know. He got the call. Directing a film with that Macaroon Diaz.

TOM. *Cameron* Diaz.

ALAN. Lovely pair of gnashers. He told me the name –

TOM. *Annihilation*. Open brackets. *End of the World*. Close brackets.

ALAN. It's about robots.

TOM. Androids.

ALAN. Same difference.

TOM. What if he forgets us?

ALAN. Forget us. Forgets *me*.

TOM. If it's successful.

ALAN. Listen – I said this to David – people don't wanna see robots. They wanna see *real* people. Like them. Like us. Like *me*.

ALAN *gets up and walks around.*

I've got four hundred people working for me now. Not machines. People. *Homeworkers*. Making knickers with their hands. Won us the contract with M&S. 'Hand-finished knickers,' they said. 'That's a good idea. That's what we want.' All this internet shopping. It's just a fad. People wanna go into shops and touch before they buy. Robots aren't taking over the world. Manufacturing isn't dying. As my mum used to say – 'Alan, people will always need plates.'

Beat.

TOM. Maureen Lipman said that.

ALAN. What?

TOM. In an advert.

ALAN. Are you sure?

TOM. When her grandson got an O-Level in Pottery. She said, 'Anthony, people will always need plates.'

ALAN. Well, maybe they both said it.

TOM. She definitely said it.

Should we ask one of the runners if David's –

TOM *goes to get up*. ALAN *sits him down*.

ALAN. Hands, Tom. That's what I'm talking about. My sister, right, she used to sew sequins onto dresses. For these schmuttah houses in Great Portland Street. She did it from home. In the evenings. Thousands of these little, tiny sequins to make a bit of extra money. I'd wake up in the middle of the night, and she'd still be at it. I'd stand by her door. Watch her squinting, trying to thread the needle. More often than not she'd tell me to piss off back to bed. But sometimes… Well, sometimes she let me thread the needle for her. Now there are four hundred people who thread needles for me.

You've gotta be pleased for other people's success. David's where he is because of us. His success is our success. Well, *my* success.

How's your screenplay coming along?

TOM *shifts around uncomfortably and conceals his envelope.*

TOM. Fine.

ALAN. Still haven't finished it.

TOM. Yes. No. Yes. I –

ALAN. Make your mind up.

TOM. It's just the ending.

ALAN. Gonna be a very long ending.

TOM. I want to get it right.

ALAN. Don't drive yourself mad.

TOM. I'm not.

ALAN. Remember what happened –

TOM. David said he'd help me.

ALAN. David?

TOM. He told me to bring it along and he'd take it with him. To Hollywood.

ALAN. He can't do that.

TOM. You just said his success was our success.

ALAN. He can't change your life.

TOM. But he already has. He's irrevocably changed my life. Because of this programme.

ALAN. He's pulling your leg.

TOM. Why would he do that?

ALAN. To get you here.

TOM. He wouldn't.

ALAN. Trust me. You don't wanna speak to David.

ALAN clocks the envelope.

Is that it? Is that your film?

TOM. Yes.

ALAN. So what's it about?

TOM. Nothing.

ALAN. Well, it's gotta be about something.

TOM. You wouldn't understand.

ALAN. You think I don't know how to watch a film? We've got the hugest television you've ever seen in our lounge. Forty-two inches. Makes Cameron Diaz's teeth look like the bloody Himalayas.

Give us a look.

TOM. No.

ALAN. Just a few pages.

TOM. You'll get it out of order.

ALAN. Come on. Twenty-one years I've been waiting for this. So has the nation. We all wanna know what it's about.

TOM. It's not for *you*.

ALAN. Fine. Keep it to yourself. *My* part.

Silence.

What car do you reckon they've given Princess?

TOM. Her name's Catherine.

ALAN. Sixty million people know her as 'Princess'.

TOM. She doesn't like it.

ALAN. It's her nickname.

TOM. Because of you.

ALAN. It's a term of endearment.

TOM. It's disrespectful.

ALAN. I have a deep respect for women. I grew up in a house full of women… My sister used to hold my hand and walk me down –

TOM. Petticoat Lane. Yes. I know.

ALAN. Right. So don't tell me I'm being disrespectful, Tom.

Beat.

Any women in your life?

TOM. That's private.

ALAN. Gay private?

TOM. Private private.

ALAN. Bad, was it?

TOM. What?

ALAN. Did she break your heart?

TOM. I really don't want to talk about it.

Beat.

ALAN. It's good to talk. My mum used to say that. Alan, don't keep things bottled up. It's good to talk.

TOM *takes in a deep breath.*

It's good to talk.

TOM, *agitated, starts checking through the pages of his screenplay.*

I'm so lucky with Toni. Eighteen years of marriage, haven't gone a day without speaking to each other. Except once. *Twice.* It was a misunderstanding – she got the wrong end of the stick. Anyway, I knew straight away. She was the one. That moment she walked into the shop. A chance in a million. I could have been at the factory or with another customer. But I was standing by the till marking down some stockings – they were seconds – and she walked in. The moment was there and I grabbed it with both hands. Well, one hand –

TOM (*overlapping*). …and a pricing gun.

ALAN. – and a pricing gun. Exactly.

He looks at TOM, *who is still checking through his screenplay.*

You should have asked Princess out while you had the chance.

TOM. I'm missing thirty-five.

ALAN. What happened with you two?

TOM. *Alan…* I don't have thirty-five! Page thirty-five is missing.

ALAN. Okay. Calm down.

TOM. It was here.

ALAN. Maybe it's out of order.

TOM. Impossible.

ALAN. Check.

TOM. I *have* checked. *I know how to put things in order.* I'm an archivist. It was here. After thirty-four, and before thirty-six.

ALAN. All right. Keep your knickers on.

TOM. What have you done with it?

ALAN. What do you mean, what have I done with it?

TOM. You've got it, haven't you?

ALAN. Don't start accusing me.

TOM. You've done it to sabotage me.

ALAN. Don't be ridiculous.

TOM. Make me look stupid.

ALAN. Well –

TOM. Empty your pockets.

ALAN. What?

TOM. Empty them!

ALAN. What is this, the Dreyfus Affair?

Maybe you dropped it.

TOM. Where? Where could I drop it?

ALAN. Calm down.

TOM. My life's work.

ALAN. You don't want David to see you like this.

TOM. It's a disaster.

ALAN. Fax him another copy.

TOM. You have no idea about the writing process.

ALAN. Christ.

ALAN *gets down on his knees and starts looking under the sofa.*

TOM. Everyone's going to think I'm a failure.

ALAN. You just… breathe… yeah.

TOM *breathes*.

TOM. I'm not sure about this, Alan.

ALAN. In out. In out.

TOM. I mean the programme.

ALAN *pulls himself up, and sits down next to* TOM.

ALAN. Seven years old – you're this high, standing by the food table. Remember, David gave us tea afterwards. Catherine in her posh party frock. Me and her. Stuffing our faces. And you're just staring at the food. Wouldn't eat a thing. You were so stiff. And well-dressed. I thought you looked like that collection box. You know, the Barnardo's boy with the callipers. Only without the callipers. And the eye patch. Jesus. He was an unlucky bastard. Anyway, same slicked-down hair and jumper.

TOM. I wanted an egg-mayonnaise sandwich.

ALAN. You should have had one.

TOM. Someone ate them all.

ALAN. Not *all* of them.

TOM. No. You put some in your pocket.

ALAN. For later… I loved egg-mayonnaise. What a day.

Catherine showed me her knickers.

TOM. Catherine showed *me* her knickers.

ALAN. If you insist.

TOM. They were white. With butterflies on them.

ALAN. Don't you wish you were seven again?

TOM. Not really.

Beat.

ALAN. You get letters, don't you, Tom?

TOM. Yes.

ALAN. Do you?

TOM. A few.

ALAN. Really? How many?

TOM. I don't know.

ALAN. Roughly.

TOM. About ten.

ALAN. A year?

TOM. A week.

ALAN. Oh. Right.

TOM. More around Christmas. I get a lot that time of year.

ALAN. You see. That's nice, isn't it. Coz they feel sorry for
you. I get hundreds. Mainly begging. But that happens when
you're successful. I'm sure Richard Branson has to deal with
it all the time. It's double-edged. Every seven years, I'm
blasted into forty million homes. Every seven years my
underwear's in people's faces.

TOM. Forty million?

ALAN. Give or take. It goes up every seven years. I mean,
when I was seven we didn't even have a TV.

TOM. Forty million.

ALAN. Before video sales. Did you know I'm very big in
Japan?

TOM. Oh God.

ALAN. It's understandable. People wanna see where we are.
They wanna feel my success. Your disappointment.
Catherine's legs. You, me, Catherine. We're their kids too.

The nation expects, Tom.

TOM. I can't do this.

ALAN. Honestly, you worry too much. Always have.

TOM. I really mean it this time. I can't go through with it.

ALAN. Like the last time. And the time before that. And the
time before that. You heard about the boy who put his finger
in a dyke –

TOM. I don't want to do it!

ALAN. Not interested.

TOM. I can't sleep. I wake up earlier and earlier. It's hardly worth my while putting on pyjamas. Last week I mixed a whole batch of *Evening Stars* with the *Evening Standards*. No wonder I'm losing bits of paper. I can't concentrate knowing it's always there. This albatross.

ALAN. What?

TOM. I shot an albatross when I was seven. It constantly haunts me.

ALAN. Did you?

TOM. It's an allegory.

ALAN. Right.

TOM. This constant watching. I can't take it any more.

ALAN. It's only every seven years.

TOM. No it's not. It's always there. Hanging around my neck. Like a noose.

ALAN. You're not gonna start talking about death, are you.

TOM. We have to sit here and be judged. By everybody. And no one cares how we feel about it.

ALAN. David cares.

TOM. I don't know if he does.

ALAN. You wanna see David, don't you?

TOM. I don't know who to trust any more.

ALAN. And Catherine? When she eventually graces us with her presence.

TOM *is silent*.

You always used to get on so well.

It's like a reunion. The three of us. The kids. Lower. Middle.
Upper. We're ambassadors of our class. If you don't do it,
the programme won't go ahead. They need all three of us.
Without you – there's no middle. No medium. No average.
You don't wanna disappoint people, do you, Tom?

TOM. The expectation.

ALAN. But that's the brilliant thing about you, Tom. Nobody
expects anything of you.

Beat. TOM *lets this statement settle. Then the sound of faint
clapping outside.*

Hang on –

ALAN *gets up.*

BMW. Heels. Tights. Legs. It's Princess. Princess has
arrived. Of course they bring her in a BMW. I mean, look at
the Royal Family – they're more German than English.

He wolf-whistles down.

Forty-two, she's still got the loveliest legs. Here we go…

He looks at TOM, *who is sitting very stiffly.*

It's Catherine, Tom.

Look at you, all stiff… Listen. Don't feel bad about the
albatross – you were *seven*. Let it go.

ALAN *goes over to* TOM, *and ruffles his hair.* TOM
smoothes it down.

TOM. Don't do that.

ALAN. What… This?

ALAN *ruffles* TOM's *hair again.* TOM *pushes* ALAN's
hand away. ALAN *pushes* TOM's *shoulder, jokingly.*

That's it. Good. You've gotta toughen yourself up. Barnardo
Boy.

ALAN taps TOM's face lightly.

TOM. Stop it!

TOM reactively hits ALAN back quite hard.

ALAN. Ouch. That hurt.

TOM. I told you to stop it.

ALAN slaps him round the head. TOM punches ALAN in the stomach.

ALAN. You little bastard.

ALAN launches himself at TOM.

TOM. *You're* the bastard.

They wrestle. ALAN grabs hold of TOM by his jumper. TOM pulls away.

Let go.

ALAN. I'll let go when you calm down.

TOM. I am calm.

ALAN. You're winding yourself up.

TOM. I'm calm!

ALAN. You're getting yourself into a...

TOM. What?

ALAN. One of your...

TOM. What?

ALAN. States.

TOM. You're going to rip it.

ALAN. I'll only rip it if you keep moving.

TOM. I want to leave.

ALAN. You can't leave. David'll be here in a minute.

TOM. David's destroyed my life.

ALAN. David gave you a life.

Beat. Suddenly TOM *escapes free out of the jumper, leaving* ALAN *holding it.*

TOM. Hah. See. I'm free. I don't have to do this.

ALAN. Okay.

TOM. Okay.

I'm leaving.

ALAN. Fine.

TOM. Fine.

Beat.

ALAN. Why are you still here?

TOM. Can I have my jumper back?

ALAN. No.

TOM. Give it back.

ALAN. No.

TOM. That's my jumper.

Black.

(21)

A large '21' appears on the TV screen. Then disappears.

Lights up. The backdrop is London, circa 1980.

CATHERINE *(21) is sitting on the sofa, rolling a cigarette. She is an anarchist, with appropriate punk hairdo and ripped, baggy T-shirt. She is rather beautiful, and speaks with an upper-class accent.* ALAN *(21) is holding* TOM's *(21) jumper (a different jumper to the '42' one, but still conservative in style).* ALAN *is dressed in the same suit.*

TOM. Give it back.

CATHERINE. Give it back to him, Alan.

ALAN. I'm only having a look.

TOM. Can I have it back?

ALAN. Can I? *Can* I?

CATHERINE. Alan, stop being such a fascist.

ALAN. Fascist? Me? That's a laugh.

TOM. It's mine.

ALAN. I'm checking the quality.

TOM. My mother knitted it.

ALAN. The unevenness. The humanity.

TOM. *May* I have it back... please?

CATHERINE. For fuck's sake. Give it back.

ALAN. All right. Keep yer knickers on.

    ALAN *throws* TOM *back the jumper.*

    (To TOM.) You've got something stuck to your shoe.

    TOM *picks his heel up and looks behind.*

'Hello Sailor.'

Isn't he good? You're pure entertainment.

CATHERINE. Alan, leave Tom alone.

ALAN. Just having a joke. He's like a brother to me. Aren't you, Tommy?

TOM. Tom.

ALAN. And you're like a sister to me, Princess.

CATHERINE *rolls her eyes at* TOM. TOM *half-smiles back.*

Not *my* sister, obviously. You're nothing like my actual sister. For a start, you've got long legs. And a *waist*. And much bigger breasts.

TOM. Alan!

ALAN. What? It's my job.

CATHERINE *walks downstage and looks out front.*

CATHERINE. Where the fuck is David?

TOM. He's coming.

ALAN. I've never been a breast man.

CATHERINE. We could just film it ourselves. (*Re: camera.*) How does this work?

TOM. It's David's.

CATHERINE. Don't you think this is all a bit pervy? Filming us. Bit kinky.

TOM. No.

ALAN. Shut up, Tom. Keep talking.

CATHERINE. He asked me what I was going to wear.

TOM. Me too.

ALAN. And me.

CATHERINE. Told me I was cameragenic.

ALAN. What does that mean?

CATHERINE. He probably wants to sleep with me.

ALAN. Filthy sod.

CATHERINE *lights her cigarette*.

TOM. Is that marijuana?

CATHERINE. Just a boring fag.

Do you want one?

ALAN. He is one.

TOM. I don't smoke.

ALAN. Smoking'll kill you?

CATHERINE. Who cares? I'm going to die young anyway.

ALAN. Don't say that.

CATHERINE. I want to die before I'm forty. Just like Sid.

Vicious.

ALAN *spits. They look at him*.

Sure you don't want a drag?

TOM. No. Thank you.

CATHERINE *smiles*.

ALAN. So what exactly do you do in Oxbridge?

TOM. Cambridge.

CATHERINE. He studies.

TOM. I read English.

ALAN. Well, I can do that. We can all do that.

TOM. Can you?

CATHERINE. He's in the top two per cent of the country.

ALAN. That's funny. Coz he's meant to be average. He's meant to be your bog-standard somewhere-in-the-middle.

CATHERINE. Education frees.

ALAN. Well, it's not free for me, is it. He's costing me a bloody fortune.

CATHERINE. In seven years he'll be running the country.

ALAN. He'll be a bloody civil servant.

CATHERINE. How do you know?

ALAN. Coz none of your lot give us a look-in.

CATHERINE. What do you mean by 'my lot'?

ALAN. The haves. The toffs. The BBC.

TOM. We're not on the BBC.

CATHERINE. We've got to prove them wrong. That's why we're here.

TOM. We're on ITV.

CATHERINE. To fuck up the fascist regime. Isn't that right, Tom?

TOM. I've got to finish my dissertation.

ALAN. He's got to finish his dissertation.

TOM *holds his envelope. They look at him.*

TOM. It's just the conclusion.

CATHERINE. You brought it with you?

TOM. I thought I could work on it. On the way here. On the train. But... I can't write on trains. I get motion sickness.

CATHERINE. What's it about?

ALAN. He was a sickly kid.

TOM. Nothing.

CATHERINE. Go on. Tell me.

TOM. No –

CATHERINE. I might be able to help.

TOM (*hesitates*). Keats.

ALAN. Who?

TOM. John Keats. He's a poet.

ALAN. I know him.

TOM. No, you don't.

ALAN. John Keats. He's from the East End.

TOM. Don't be ridiculous.

CATHERINE. I love Keats.

TOM. Do you?

ALAN. His dad worked in the stables.

TOM. No. He didn't.

ALAN. He did.

TOM. He didn't, Alan.

ALAN. Please yourself.

> CATHERINE *has picked up the dissertation and reads the title on the front.*

CATHERINE. 'Keats – Perfectionist or Nihilist.' Is that the title?

TOM. Please don't touch it. It's in order.

CATHERINE. Perfectionist, or nihilist. Aren't they the same thing?

TOM. No.

CATHERINE. Well, they are.

TOM. They're not.

CATHERINE. Nothing's perfect.

TOM. That's a cliché.

CATHERINE. If anything, Keats was an anarchist.

TOM. He was not.

CATHERINE. That's what you should put at the end – 'Keats was an anarchist. So fuck the lot of you.'

TOM. You can't say that.

CATHERINE. Why not?

TOM. You've got to substantiate it with a quote. 'Beauty is truth, truth beauty – that is all ye know on earth, and all ye need to know.' 'Ode on a Grecian Urn'.

CATHERINE *sings an in-yer-face punk rendition of 'Ever Fallen in Love' by The Buzzcocks.*

When she stops singing, ALAN *and* TOM *are looking at her.*

CATHERINE. Buzzcocks.

ALAN *hands* TOM *a business card from his jacket pocket.*

TOM (*reading*). 'For all shapes of bums,
        Thighs, legs and tums,
        Your nanny, your granny, your sisters and mums –
        No one shifts a pair of knickers like Alan Morris.'

ALAN (*overlapping*). Alan Morris.

TOM. '*Knickers to You.* 168 Commercial Road.'

ALAN. Now that's poetry.

CATHERINE. I thought you had a stall?

He hands her a card.

ALAN. I've expanded. Got a girl who works for me. Toni. She's great. Toni could flog a dead horse to a jockey. Got an eye for design. She does amazing things with the window display. Like artwork, it is. And she keeps herself nice. Which is good for business.

CATHERINE *goes to hand back the card.*

Keep it.

CATHERINE. Erm… Thank you.

ALAN. Would you like a job?

CATHERINE. With you?

ALAN. Yes.

CATHERINE. No, thank you.

ALAN. Come on. Women work now. We got a lady running this country. Well… *woman.* You could get yourself some nice clothes.

CATHERINE. I'm not interested.

ALAN. Don't turn your nose up. It's a classy establishment.

TOM. She's not interested.

ALAN. Education's all well and good. But it doesn't feed ya. It doesn't clothe ya. What you gonna do with that degree, Tom?

TOM. Well –

ALAN. University of Life, me. And look at how I'm doing.

TOM. I haven't decided yet.

ALAN. Twenty-one, and you still don't know what you wanna do? What you gonna say to David?

TOM. He might not ask.

ALAN. Of course he'll ask.

TOM. I don't know.

ALAN. Gotta have an answer.

TOM (*to* CATHERINE). What about you?

ALAN. She'll have a couple of kids.

CATHERINE. I don't want children.

ALAN. Course you do. All women want children.

CATHERINE. Well, I don't.

TOM. Neither do I.

CATHERINE. See... Tom doesn't want them either.

TOM. Malthus was right.

CATHERINE. There's no future.

ALAN. Well, I can understand Tom. Look at him when he was seven. But you, Princess. You're gorgeous. Think about it... Your looks. My chutzpah.

CATHERINE. *I certainly don't want children with you.* I want to have a band. Like Siouxsie Sioux.

TOM. Really?

CATHERINE. I don't play an instrument. My parents should never have let me give up the harp.

ALAN. Hang on. Doesn't that Siouxsie Sioux wear swastikas?

CATHERINE. So?

ALAN. Don't you think that's racist?

CATHERINE. She's being ironic.

ALAN. I suppose Hitler was being ironic.

CATHERINE. In a way. Yes.

ALAN. He murdered millions of people.

CATHERINE. You've got to question things, Alan. You've got to challenge the status quo.

ALAN. That's exactly what Hitler said.

CATHERINE. You're so blinded by the system.

ALAN. Am I?

CATHERINE. Thatcher's minion.

ALAN. She's right about those Russians –

CATHERINE. Your success is built on other people's misery.

ALAN. I sell smalls.

CATHERINE. The suppression of the unions is a disgrace.

ALAN. What do you know about the unions?

CATHERINE. I stand on picket lines.

ALAN. You just wanna piss off your parents.

CATHERINE. No. I don't.

ALAN. Yeah. You do.

CATHERINE. I do not.

ALAN. What do they make of all this?

CATHERINE. I don't care.

ALAN. Are they happy their daughter's wearing schmuttahs?

CATHERINE. I can do what I want. I'm an adult.

ALAN. Still living off Daddy's allowance?

CATHERINE. Fuck you, Alan.

ALAN. All that money I pay to the Royal Family. That's how you speak to me.

CATHERINE. My family aren't royal.

ALAN (*motioning to* TOM). Taxes so he can sit on his arse all day and read books.

CATHERINE. I don't care what you think of me. Your precon-
ceived notions of who I am. Or what I should be. Because of
whom my parents are. Is it *whom* or *who*?

TOM. Whom.

CATHERINE. Thought so.

ALAN. I think you do care.

TOM. Though you can say who –

ALAN. I think you care a lot.

CATHERINE. It really upsets you, doesn't it? That I don't give
a fuck about money. That I have no respect for it. That I
don't fulfil your stupid expectations.

ALAN. You're wearing white, cotton knickers.

Beat.

CATHERINE. No, I'm not.

ALAN. You are.

CATHERINE. I am not.

ALAN. With a small bow in the middle.

CATHERINE. Actually, I'm not wearing any.

ALAN. Prove it.

TOM. Alan!

CATHERINE. That'd give you something to think about for the
next seven years, wouldn't it.

They all stare at each other.

ALAN. Can you feel that?

CATHERINE. What?

ALAN. The tension.

CATHERINE. I beg your pardon?

ALAN. Come on. Admit it, Princess. There's all this tension between us.

CATHERINE. There is no tension between us.

TOM. I think I want to write a film.

ALAN. All right. Not tension. Just Tom.

TOM. I think that's what I want to do. When David asks what I'm going to do. I'll say that. I think.

CATHERINE. That's a brilliant idea.

TOM. Really?

ALAN. A film?

TOM. Yes.

ALAN. Like you see at the pictures?

TOM (*to* CATHERINE). Do you really think so?

CATHERINE. Absolutely.

ALAN. How do you do that then?

TOM. What?

ALAN. How do you write a film?

TOM. Well, I suppose you have an idea, a story, and then you write it.

ALAN. Like with Steve McQueen and all that? You're doing one of those?

TOM. Yes.

ALAN. I love Steve McQueen. And you'll get him cheap. He hasn't done anything good since *Towering Inferno*. That bit at the end when he gets dropped by the helicopter.

TOM. I don't want to write about helicopters –

ALAN. Or I could get Helen Shapiro for you. She's from the East End. My mum used to know her. (*Sings*.) 'Walking back to happiness...'

CATHERINE. What's the story?

TOM. I'm not sure yet.

ALAN. I've got plenty of stories.

CATHERINE. We know.

ALAN. You want one of mine?

TOM. Not particularly.

ALAN. There's one about when I was a kid – (*Laughs*.) Nah. I've got an even better one than that – (*He stops*.) Actually, I could just write the film myself.

TOM. No, you couldn't.

ALAN. Course I could.

TOM. You couldn't.

ALAN. You said you just need an idea.

TOM. It takes a bit more than that.

ALAN. Worried it's better than yours?

TOM. You can't even construct a sentence.

ALAN. You having a dig? I think he's having a dig. What kind of stories have you got anyway?

CATHERINE. He's got stories. Haven't you, Tom?

ALAN. What's it about? Train journeys from London to Cambridge.

TOM. Maybe.

ALAN. Fascinating.

TOM. To some people it is.

ALAN. Some people might consider that boring.

TOM. My life is not boring.

ALAN. Why – do you take the slow train to Ely and change on the way?

TOM. What if I do?

ALAN. I'm not gonna go to the pictures and watch it.

CATHERINE. Well, you don't have to.

ALAN. And Steve McQueen won't do it.

TOM. How do you know?

ALAN. Coz the man drives a car. He doesn't get trains.

TOM. It's not about *trains*.

ALAN. And neither will Helen Shapiro, coz she *walked* back to happiness. She didn't catch the 2:19 from Ely.

TOM. It's not about bloody trains!

Beat.

CATHERINE. I'll go and watch it.

ALAN. Don't you think David's gonna have something to say about this?

TOM. Why?

ALAN. Kind of his territory, isn't it?

CATHERINE. David can't interfere with our choices. That's the point. It's a documentary about our lives.

ALAN. You're just trying to copy him.

TOM. He does television programmes. Not films.

ALAN. Same difference.

TOM. No. It's not. Television's ugly. It's about ugly people with ugly lives. There's no beauty or truth in it. It's not art. It's mediocre, mind-numbing, opiate for the masses.

CATHERINE. Fuck TV.

ALAN. You wait till I tell David what you just said.

Beat. ALAN *walks over to the sofa. To* TOM.

(*To* TOM.) Budge over.

TOM *doesn't move.*

Tom. Move.

TOM. I can't.

ALAN. Come on.

TOM. *I can't.* I can't move my legs.

CATHERINE. Are you all right?

ALAN. Stop mucking about.

TOM. I just need to be left alone.

CATHERINE. Are you unwell?

ALAN. I wanna sit down. Budge over.

CATHERINE. Stop it, Alan.

ALAN. There's nothing wrong with him.

CATHERINE. Are you okay?

TOM. I shouldn't have come.

CATHERINE. Tom –

TOM. I was sitting on the train platform, and I had this… heaviness. Everything's very heavy. Can you feel that? Like the sky's pushing down and you're sinking into the ground.

CATHERINE *nods.*

I thought I should go back. Just forget the programme. But I went to get up. My legs didn't work. My heart's thumping. I can feel it in my throat. My ears.

CATHERINE. Tom –

TOM. Usually it stops. Eventually.

CATHERINE. Do you want me to get David?

TOM *closes his eyes and breathes.*

TOM. Butterflies.

CATHERINE *looks at* ALAN. *He shrugs.*

CATHERINE. Tom?

TOM. There was a butterfly on the train platform. It had eyes on its wings. I watched it fly past and my heart slowed down. Then it flew back. Lands next to me. On the bench. Opens its wings. I was watching it. Opening and closing its wings. It's perfect. A beautiful rainbow of perfect symmetry. The chest pain disappeared. My heart slowed down. And then there's a voice – 'It's you, isn't it? You're that boy. That seven-year-old. Off the telly.' I try to ignore him. 'It *is* you. I know it is.' And suddenly the butterfly's gone, and I think, you idiot. Do you realise what you've just done? Somewhere there's going to be a hurricane because of you. You've changed the course of history. Of my life. Because of this programme. And I look up and everyone on the platform is staring at me.

CATHERINE *and* ALAN *are staring at him.*

I want to be remembered for something. Something other than this programme.

Beat.

ALAN. Have you ever had your chest measured?

CATHERINE. Go and see where David is.

ALAN. 34D. I'm right, aren't I? It's like a gift.

CATHERINE. Alan –

ALAN. I'm just saying, most women wear the wrong-sized
    bra –

CATHERINE. For crying out loud.

ALAN. It might give you some shape –

Suddenly, CATHERINE *pulls up her top and flashes her
breasts at* ALAN. *She is not wearing a bra. She pulls her top
back down. A moment's silence.*

Black.

(42)

A large '42' appears on the TV screen. Then disappears.

Lights up. The TV is again a window.

CATHERINE *(42) sits in the same stage-left position on the
sofa as before. She is neat and has a handbag next to her. She is
applying lipstick.* ALAN *(42) sits stage-right of the sofa.* TOM
*(42) sits awkwardly in the middle of the sofa. He clutches his
manuscript.*

CATHERINE. How are the children?

ALAN. Great. Great. Sophie's great. We're choosing
    universities.

CATHERINE. We're not quite there yet. Thomas is fifteen.
    Henry's twelve.

ALAN. You've got all that to come.

CATHERINE. Yes.

ALAN. It's a worry.

CATHERINE. Well, they both board now, so I suppose I should be used to them being away. Geoffrey's idea. It's his Alma Mater.

ALAN. His what?

CATHERINE. His old school.

ALAN. I couldn't send them to my old school – they'd come out speaking Punjabi. If you want the best, you gotta pay for it. Education. Education. Education. As my mum used to say.

CATHERINE. Indeed.

ALAN. Sophie's gonna be the first person in my family to go to university.

CATHERINE. You must be very proud.

ALAN. Yes. We are.

CATHERINE. What's she going to do?

ALAN. Fine Art and Textiles. She wants to be a fashion designer. Personally, I think she'd be a great lawyer.

CATHERINE. Thomas wants to be an officer in the army.

ALAN. As long as the child is happy.

TOM. Catherine, can I speak to you for a second?

ALAN. Did you know you can get a degree in knitting? Knitting, for Christ's sake. She puts things together. These outfits. I mean, I think she looks like she got dressed in the dark. But what do I know? I still use the same tailor who made my bar mitzvah suit. Once in a while I get an Armani. I like the way they're cut. What do you think?

He shows off the suit. She looks.

CATHERINE. I like the shirt.

TOM (*to* CATHERINE). Just a word in private, before David –

ALAN. I give her money to buy clothes. Can't bear the thought of her walking around in all that second-hand, Camden Market crap. But that's the fashion, she says.

CATHERINE. How's your son?

ALAN. Daniel? Fine. Struggling a bit at school.

CATHERINE. Really?

ALAN. It's nothing.

CATHERINE. Not being bullied I hope?

ALAN. What? No. My son. The other way round if anything.

TOM *shakes his head in disbelief.*

He's not very good at spelling. Now they call it dyslexic. All of a sudden everything's a disease. Attention deficit. Seasonal disorder. It's raining. Get over it. So he can't spell. He's very good with numbers. He can do Business Studies.

TOM. You don't believe in further education.

ALAN. Yes I do.

TOM. You said you didn't believe in it.

ALAN. What you talking about?

TOM. You believe in the '*University of Life*'. That's what you said.

ALAN. Don't tell me what I do and don't believe in.

TOM. That's what he said, isn't it?

CATHERINE. My memory's fucked.

TOM. Run back the programmes. You'll see.

CATHERINE. Geoffrey's been on at me to do memory exercises. I forgot his dry cleaning last week.

TOM. You mocked me. About my degree. You said it was all a waste of time.

CATHERINE. Personally, I blame the drugs.

ALAN. Well, it has been, hasn't it? You didn't even finish.

TOM. I wasn't *well*.

ALAN. Please.

CATHERINE. Can you two behave, or do I have to knock your heads together?

Beat.

ALAN. I bet you're a wonderful mother. Firm... Fair... Sexy.

CATHERINE. Thank you.

ALAN. Look at her, Tom. Forty-two, and still as sexy as she was when she was fourteen. I mean, twenty-one.

CATHERINE. Cut it out, Alan.

ALAN. Look after yourself, don't you?

CATHERINE. Not particularly.

ALAN. Geoffrey looks after you though, doesn't he. Makes sure you don't go without.

CATHERINE. Yes. He works very hard.

ALAN. Still tax-dodging in Switzerland?

CATHERINE. He *works* in Switzerland during the week, yes.

ALAN. If you don't mind me asking, Princess. What exactly do you do with yourself?

CATHERINE. Sorry?

ALAN. During the week. No husband. No kids. What do you do?

CATHERINE. Oh, absolutely nothing, Alan. When I can be bothered, I sleep with the gardener.

ALAN. Really?

CATHERINE. I do a lot of volunteer work. Mainly animal. I'm on the board of a donkey sanctuary.

TOM. Catherine, I'd really like to have a word –

ALAN. We used to go riding on donkeys round Hampstead Heath. I wonder what happened to 'em.

CATHERINE. They probably died from exhaustion.

ALAN. You trust him, do ya?

CATHERINE. Excuse me?

ALAN. Geoffrey. Being away all that time.

CATHERINE. Well, of course I trust him.

ALAN. Oh. No. Don't get me wrong. I'm sure he's totally legit. I mean, look at me… I'd never cheat on Toni. *Never*. But she still wants the final say on the au pair. You get photos with the applications. She basically rules out all the ones I tick.

CATHERINE. You've got an au pair?

TOM. Catherine –

ALAN. Not for me. For Toni and the kids. Lovely girl at the moment. From Poland. Lenka. Zenka. Shiksa. Something like that. I was telling her my grandparents were Polish. Arrived here with no English and a sewing machine. I think it must be nice for her. You know. To see what she could aspire to. Money. Democracy.

A house in Bushey.

TOM. Hang on. Poland *is* a democracy.

ALAN. Is it?

TOM. Yes.

ALAN. Well, it wasn't *then*. It was full of bastard Cossacks.

CATHERINE. I'm not sure if I could trust an au pair. Charles became very friendly with theirs. He took her away skiing with him and the boys. I always found that rather odd.

ALAN. Who?

CATHERINE. Prince of Wales.

ALAN. Oh.

TOM *stands up*.

TOM. Catherine!

CATHERINE. Yes. What is it, Tom?

TOM *looks at* ALAN.

TOM. Nothing.

ALAN. Oh. Don't mind me.

CATHERINE. Go on.

TOM. It's just, erm –

ALAN. Pretend I'm not here.

CATHERINE. Come on. Spit it out.

TOM. It's good to see you, Catherine.

CATHERINE. Well, it's good to be here. Geoffrey hates it, of course. The intrusion. He finds it all very uncouth. He disappears when David comes around to do the home interview.

ALAN. Toni liked it at first. Now, not so much.

CATHERINE. He actually filmed me eating muesli. He told me to do something I usually do in the morning, so I did that.

ALAN. He wants you to be exactly as you are.

CATHERINE. Except I had to eat five bowls of it because of all the different camera angles.

ALAN. And television makes you look fatter – have you noticed that?

TOM. Catherine, I'm sorry, I have to tell you something –

ALAN. Come on, Tommy. Don't start all this again.

TOM. I wanted to explain.

CATHERINE. What's wrong?

ALAN. He's saying he doesn't want to do the programme.

TOM. I wanted to speak to you. Alone.

ALAN. Don't let me stop you.

TOM. Can't you see? We're being exploited. Our lives are being exploited.

CATHERINE. I'm not being exploited.

ALAN. No one's being exploited.

TOM. Said the man who uses slave labour.

ALAN. *Homeworkers*.

CATHERINE. What's got into you, Tom?

ALAN. I am a good employer. I could have schlepped my business off to China. Had small, unwanted Chinese girls in a sweaty factory sewing elastic into knickers, fourteen hours a day, for a fraction of the price. But I said to my accountant, Trevor, 'No.' I won't do it. I'm keeping my money here. I'm supporting the British economy. And this is good for my business.

TOM. *Your* business. Not *my* business.

ALAN. That's right. That's exactly it. You don't have a business. You have no code of conduct.

CATHERINE. You can't leave the programme, Tom. You signed a contract.

ALAN. She's right. You can't quit. You signed a contract. We all signed a contract.

TOM. I was seven!

ALAN. You can't go back on a contract. It's bad business. It's dishonest.

TOM. David came into the classroom. I thought he was the milkman. The teacher asked for volunteers. I put my hand up.

ALAN. David chose you to be part of this. You're lucky.

TOM. I wanted to be milk monitor. I didn't want this.

ALAN. You ungrateful shit.

CATHERINE. The programme won't go ahead, Tom. They need all three of us.

ALAN. You go: the whole social experiment falls apart.

TOM. This isn't a social experiment. It's pornography.

ALAN. Pornography?

TOM. Yes. Social pornography.

ALAN. Close your ears, Princess.

CATHERINE. I know what pornography is.

ALAN. So do I. This is not pornography.

TOM. It's a parasite. Sucking away at us. Can't you see it infects everything that we do? It stops us from living. Really living.

CATHERINE. Tom, please calm down.

TOM. There was an experiment. They put one single rat in a cage and put a camera on it. After a while, it changed its normal way of behaving. It stopped behaving like a rat and started playing up to camera. It was performing.

ALAN. They put monkeys in a room with a typewriter and they wrote the fucking Bible. What's your point?

CATHERINE. Actually, they wrote the Complete Works of Shakespeare.

ALAN. They did that too? Clever monkeys.

CATHERINE. It's a hypothesis.

TOM. The rat ate five bowls of muesli.

ALAN. Really?

CATHERINE. Are you calling me a rat, Tom?

TOM. They're making us look like idiots.

CATHERINE. I don't think I look like an idiot.

ALAN. Our lives make great TV.

CATHERINE. I don't care if Geoffrey and the boys think it's embarrassing. I like being on television.

TOM. I don't want my life to make great TV. I want my life to be my life. David has stolen my life.

ALAN. Without him you'd be even more of a nobody.

TOM. That's not true.

ALAN. I'm sorry. Is somebody speaking?

TOM. I've finally made something of myself.

ALAN. Your life's shit. It stinks. Guess what, that's entertainment.

TOM. I finished the film. Nearly finished.

ALAN. What – this?

He picks up the screenplay.

TOM. Don't touch it. It's in order.

ALAN. The longest film in Hollywood history. What is it – *Shoah*?

TOM. Give it back, Alan.

ALAN. David's not gonna do it now.

TOM. He owes me.

ALAN. Owes *you*? I carry this programme. If anything, he owes *me*.

TOM. Look at yourself, Alan. Take a long, hard look at those tapes. You're so blind you can't even see it.

CATHERINE. Can you both stop this!

TOM. Have you ever thought how you come across?

CATHERINE. Do I have to get David?

ALAN. What you see is what you get.

TOM. What about the additional charges? Supplements. VAT.

ALAN. What's he on about?

TOM. Money this. Money that.

ALAN. You're being ridiculous. And if I might say, a little bit racist.

TOM. Everyone's laughing at you. Behind your back. At your new money.

CATHERINE. Tom, calm down.

ALAN. *Butterflies*.

> TOM *launches himself at* ALAN *and tries to grab the screenplay. A short struggle.*

TOM. Give it back.

ALAN. Get off.

CATHERINE. Wait until David gets here. You'll be in huge trouble. Both of you.

ALAN. He started it.

TOM. Let go –

> ALAN *feels a twinge in his knee. And screams out in pain.*

ALAN. You –

> ALAN *sits down.*

CATHERINE. What's wrong?

ALAN. Him. Goering. *He's* wrong.

TOM. You fell into a bunker. You clown.

ALAN. My money's as good as anybody's. Twenty-one years ago that club wouldn't have let me in. Nobody's gonna make me feel like a second-class citizen. Not now. Not ever.

TOM. Let go of the Holocaust, Alan.

ALAN. What did you just say?

CATHERINE. Tom, what's happening to you?

ALAN. He's a nutcase.

TOM. What's happened to *me*?

ALAN. He needs locking up.

TOM. Boarding schools, muesli, a house in Kensington. That's your idea of 'fucking up the system'?

CATHERINE. I live in Fulham.

TOM. I stayed true to myself.

CATHERINE. You've never finished a thing.

TOM. I stuck to my guns.

CATHERINE. Your degree, your film –

TOM. You said you wanted to be dead by the time you were forty.

   ALAN *spits*.

CATHERINE. Well, I'm sorry I didn't live up to expectation.

   ALAN *spits*.

TOM. So am I!

   CATHERINE *slaps* TOM *hard across the face*.

   Black.

(21)

Quick scene change. A large '21' appears on the TV screen. Then disappears.

Lights up.

ALAN *(21) slaps* TOM *(21) hard across the face.*

TOM. What did you do that for!

ALAN. I'm trying to snap you out of it.

TOM. Get off me.

Beat.

ALAN. Oh. I see what you're doing.

TOM. What?

ALAN. Very clever.

TOM *looks at him blankly.*

'Keats' this. 'Grecian Urn' that.

TOM. I don't know what you're talking about.

ALAN. See. You're moving now. You're fine now.

TOM. I don't feel fine.

ALAN. Playing the victim.

TOM. No, I'm not.

ALAN. She's fallen for it, hook, line and sinker.

Beat.

TOM. Has she?

ALAN. Oh. Yeah. She's lapping it up.

TOM. She is?

ALAN. You gonna ask her out then?

TOM. What?

ALAN. She's up for it.

TOM. No, she's not.

ALAN. So you're not gonna ask her out.

TOM. No.

ALAN. All right then. I'll ask her out.

TOM. You can't.

ALAN. Why not?

TOM. We're not allowed to meet outside the programme.

ALAN. Gotta grab those opportunities, Tom.

TOM. It's against the rules.

ALAN. With both hands.

TOM. You said she fancied *me*.

ALAN. I don't think she's that picky.

TOM. She doesn't fancy you.

ALAN. How do you know?

TOM. Look at you.

ALAN. I understand women, Tommy. I grew up in a house full
    of women. Slept in the same bed as my sister. I was her little
    doll. She loved showing me off. She'd hold my hand, walk
    me down Petticoat Lane saying, 'This is Al. This is my little
    brother.' Sometimes she'd take me to the sweet stall by
    Aldgate, show Peanut Harry her knickers in exchange for a
    sherbet dab. And I'd try to eat it. Still holding her hand. Ever
    tried that? Eating a sherbet dab with one hand? Bloody
    impossible. But I didn't want to let her go, you see. Coz I
    loved her. Gives you a deep respect for women. Having a
    sister. Love and respect.

    You don't have a sister, do you, Tommy?

TOM. It's *Tom*, Alan. You know my name's Tom. And you know I don't have a sister. You've known me for fourteen years. I've never had a sister. Neither do I want one. I think I want to go home –

ALAN. Watch and learn. She'll have her skirt up before you can say 'Never Mind the Bollocks'.

(42)

Quick scene change. A large '42' appears on the TV screen. Then disappears.

Lights up.

TOM. You showed me your knickers –

ALAN. Mate, I don't think now's the time.

TOM. Catherine –

CATHERINE. Tell him I'm not interested.

ALAN. She's not interested.

TOM. I didn't mean it.

CATHERINE. I don't want his apology.

ALAN. She doesn't want your apology.

TOM. I don't want you to die –

ALAN *spits*.

CATHERINE. Why on earth do you keep spitting, Alan?

ALAN. I'm warding off the evil eye.

CATHERINE. Well, stop it! You're making the floor slippery.

TOM. I meant I'm sorry that you've changed.

ALAN. I'd quit while you're behind.

CATHERINE. I haven't changed. I'm still the same person. I've just grown up.

TOM. I finished the film.

CATHERINE. Grow up, Tom.

ALAN. Nearly finished.

TOM. Can I have it back, Alan?

ALAN. Are you doing the programme or not?

TOM *goes for the screenplay.*

TOM. Give it back!

ALAN. No!

CATHERINE. Will you two shut up! You're worse than my sons. I see them one weekend in three and they're at each other's throats. Screaming and fighting. And Geoffrey just sits in the study, pretending to work when he's probably surfing porn. And who has to do the disciplining? Who's bad cop? Who screams at them to turn their music down? Their rip-off, grunge rock music. Which they think I don't get because I'm not *cool*. I was there. I heard Steve Jones do that guitar riff in '78. I listened to music so loudly my ears bled. And what I actually find offensive, what really upsets me, is that there's nothing new under the sun. Nothing. Everything's so fucking mediocre. And what I really want, what I would absolutely cream my knickers for, is for someone to come along and fucking well surprise me.

Beat. ALAN *goes up to* CATHERINE *and tries to kiss her.*

Oh. Fuck off, Alan.

She pushes him away.

TOM. I'm sorry I wasn't there, Catherine.

The station. In Cambridge.

CATHERINE. What?

TOM. I'm sorry I wasn't there to meet you.

ALAN. You arranged to meet up?

CATHERINE. I don't know what he's talking about.

TOM. I meant to be there.

ALAN. That's not allowed.

TOM. I couldn't –

ALAN. That's breaking the rules.

TOM. You said *you* were gonna ask her out.

ALAN. I was courting Toni. (*To* CATHERINE.) I was courting Toni.

CATHERINE. He's making it up.

ALAN. He's making it up.

TOM. Platform two. You must remember.

ALAN. Just wait until David hears about this.

CATHERINE. There was no meeting arranged. Tom.

TOM. Platform two. You were waiting –

CATHERINE. I wasn't.

TOM. What?

CATHERINE. I wasn't there, Tom. I really don't know what you're talking about.

TOM. Then why are you so angry with me?

CATHERINE. I'm not.

TOM. You are. You've been angry with me all this time.

CATHERINE. I'm sorry to disappoint you, but I'm not.

TOM. You see. That. There. You're angry with me.

CATHERINE. Do you want me to hit you again?

ALAN. Yes.

No. Wait. I'll do it.

CATHERINE. Why would I arrange to meet you? You could barely look at me at twenty-one.

TOM. That's not true. It's all in there.

ALAN opens the screenplay and looks at it. He hesitates.

CATHERINE. Well?

ALAN. I can't read without my specs.

TOM. He can't *read*.

ALAN. Course I can bloody read.

He attempts to read a few lines, stumbling over the longer words.

(*Reading.*) 'You suddenly look much younger... Do I?... Like a little boy.'

He looks up, embarrassed.

Where the hell's David?

ALAN throws down the screenplay and exits. Silence. CATHERINE picks it up, flicks through the pages then stops. She reads.

CATHERINE (*reading*). 'Do you think we'll ever see each other again?'

TOM. Not for years anyway.

CATHERINE (*reading*). 'The children will all be grown up.'

TOM. Couldn't I write to you once in a while?

CATHERINE (*reading*). 'No. We promised – '

TOM. I do love you. So very much. I love you with all my heart and soul.

She looks at the next page. Looks back.

CATHERINE. There's a page missing.

TOM. We did arrange to meet up. Platform two. I remember –

CATHERINE. Twenty-one years… You've got to let it go.

TOM. Easy for you to say. You got married.

CATHERINE. *You weren't there.* I was standing on that bloody platform waiting for you, arm throbbing because of this –

She pulls up her sleeve to reveal a 'Tom' tattoo on her arm.

TOM (*reading*). 'Tom.'

CATHERINE. And you never showed up.

TOM *looks at her. They are very close. Like they might kiss.*

If you stop doing this, we'll never see each other again.

TOM. Maybe we will –

CATHERINE. How?

TOM. I don't know.

Beat.

CATHERINE. This is very good. It's a lovely film. Now maybe you should move on and do something else –

TOM. David told me to bring it. If he makes my film, I'll be a success. Then… you wouldn't think I'm a failure.

CATHERINE. I don't think you're a failure. *You* think you're a failure.

TOM. Everybody thinks I'm a failure. I *am* a failure.

CATHERINE. You're not.

TOM. Don't patronise me.

CATHERINE. I'm not.

TOM. You are. You always have –

CATHERINE. That's not true.

ALAN *enters*.

ALAN. David's here. At last. He's arrived. He's in the building. Shove over.

ALAN *sits on the sofa, stage right*.

Brief Encounter.

TOM. Sorry?

ALAN. 'You suddenly look much younger… Do I?… Like a little boy.' My mum's favourite.

TOM. *Brief Encounter*?

ALAN. She was such a romantic. Not like me. I'm more of a –

TOM. Nihilist.

ALAN. Down to earth, realist. You know, David's only gone and had his teeth whitened. Thinks he's George bloody Clooney. You can show him your script now. What's it called?

TOM. *Ephemeral Moments*.

(21)

*Quick scene change. A large '21' appears on the TV screen.
Then disappears.*

Lights up.

ALAN, TOM *and* CATHERINE *are sitting on the sofa.*
CATHERINE *is smoking, sexily.* ALAN *and* TOM *stare at her,
longingly.*

CATHERINE. This is all about me, you know. Who watches this
programme? The great brainwashed. The mind-numbed
masses. They hate the upper classes. They're willing me to fall
from grace. Degrade myself. Like Princess Margaret. They'd
just love that. Well, I'm gonna really fuck it up for them. What
do you say? Should we really fuck this up for them?

ALAN. Princess –

TOM. Catherine –

She turns and exhales a plume of smoke into TOM*'s face.*

(*Shouts.*) Ah!

CATHERINE. What's wrong?

TOM. Smoke… You blew smoke in my eye.

ALAN. Jesus, a gust of wind would knock him over.

TOM. Ah –

CATHERINE. Let me have a look.

She leans over to him.

Hold still.

ALAN. This guy's a pro –

CATHERINE. Try not to rub it.

TOM. I can't see anything.

CATHERINE. Can you open it?

TOM. It stings.

CATHERINE. What if I blow on it?

TOM. Nothing.

ALAN. I take my hat off to him –

CATHERINE. Alan, can you get some water?

ALAN. I'm not thirsty.

CATHERINE. For Tom. To bathe his eye.

ALAN. Maybe you can wash his feet while you're there –

CATHERINE. Alan!

ALAN. All right, I'm going.

    ALAN *exits*.

CATHERINE. Now, stop behaving like a baby and let me have a proper look.

    CATHERINE *holds* TOM*'s face.* TOM *looks at her. They're close.*

TOM. Catherine –

CATHERINE. Yes.

TOM. I think Keats *is* from the East End. Don't tell Alan.

CATHERINE. Let me be your muse.

TOM. What?

CATHERINE. Put me in your film.

TOM. Erm –

CATHERINE. I'll write you a song. I'll get a tattoo. With your name on it.

TOM. Tattoos are dangerous.

CATHERINE. I know.

TOM. You can get blood poisoning –

CATHERINE. Let's meet up.

TOM. It's not allowed.

CATHERINE. I'll come up to Cambridge.

TOM. It's breaking the rules. David said…

CATHERINE. Screw the rules. Meet me at the station. This time next week. Platform two.

TOM. What if David finds out.

CATHERINE. He won't. Say 'yes'.

TOM. I –

   ALAN *runs in with a glass of water. He throws it in* TOM*'s face.*

CATHERINE. What the fuck are you doing?

ALAN. I'm giving him an eye bath.

CATHERINE. Tom… Are you okay?

TOM. Yes.

ALAN. David's here. I'm ready. Let's get these cameras rolling.

   He sits down.

   Here's a question: What's a Grecian urn?

   About twenty drachmas a day.

   They look at him blankly.

   Tough crowd.

   Black.

(49)

A large '49' appears on the TV screen. Then disappears.

Lights up. ALAN *and* TOM *are in exactly the same position we left them in '49'.* TOM *is wearing the jumper from '49'. Hair messy. He sits on the sofa.* ALAN *is mid-speech.*

ALAN. This isn't a mistake. That jumper is a mistake. This is a *disaster*. This is a car crash with fatalities. This is being stuck on the M25. With no turn-off in sight. And going round and round for all eternity!

TOM. You're being irrational.

ALAN. *Me?* Irrational?

TOM. Would you like some water?

ALAN. No!

I've had enough. I'm not doing the programme.

TOM. What?

ALAN. You heard me. I'm dropping out.

TOM. You can't quit now.

ALAN. Watch me.

TOM. What about the contract –

ALAN. I've got a good solicitor. He can find loopholes in the Lord's Prayer.

TOM. Is this about money?

ALAN. Well, now you mention it... do you have any idea how much Macaroon Diaz got for David's last film? Millions. And she had a stunt double for most of it.

TOM. We get paid.

ALAN. Peanuts.

TOM. For our time and inconvenience.

ALAN. What is this – clinical trials? Jury service? Do I have a stunt double? No. Who has to get up every morning? Me. Who has to sit in traffic, and sell salvaged knickers for a living? Me. *Who* tripped on a dodgy paving stone, hurt their knee, and is still waiting for compensation?

TOM. You?

ALAN. Yes. Me.

ALAN *is trying to get up, but can't.*

And while I'm here, I want all those tapes back of my interviews.

TOM. But they belong to David.

ALAN. But they're of *me*… and I want them back.

Here, help me up, will you?

TOM *goes to help him, then stops.*

TOM. I thought you hurt your knee playing golf.

Beat.

ALAN. Don't you dare tell anyone.

TOM. That's fraud.

ALAN. They need to do something about that pavement. The streets look like a bad day in Basra. Now, give us a hand.

TOM. No.

ALAN. What?

TOM. You've got to do the programme.

ALAN. I'm being serious, Tom.

TOM. So am I.

ALAN. I can't get up.

TOM. Say you'll do it.

ALAN. Stop taking the piss.

TOM. Say it!

ALAN. Fine. Fine. I'll do it.

Beat. TOM *helps him up. As soon as* ALAN*'s standing he pins* TOM *down.*

TOM. Alan –

ALAN. Mug a man when he's down, would you?

TOM. My arm –

ALAN. Have you no morals?

TOM. Get off me.

ALAN. You treacherous little shit.

TOM. All the things I've done for you, Alan.

ALAN. *Please.*

TOM. I've done the programme for you. For you and Catherine. You made me do it when I really didn't want to. And now you just want to ruin my life.

ALAN. What's to ruin?

There are cheers from a crowd outside. Clapping.

TOM. You have to do the programme, Alan.

He grabs hold of ALAN*'s legs.*

ALAN. What the –

TOM. My life depends on it.

ALAN. My knee, Tom. Get off my leg.

TOM. For the first time in my life I'm happy. Really happy. I'm a success. I have to show people that I'm a success.

ALAN. You're not a success, Tom.

TOM. I am.

ALAN. You don't even have a car!

TOM. I got married.

ALAN. What?

At that moment CATHERINE *enters. She's holding a platter of sandwiches. She looks pale, older somehow.* TOM *stands up. A moment's silence.*

CATHERINE. Hello, Alan. Tom.

ALAN. Princess.

CATHERINE. The runner gave me some sandwiches.

She puts them down. Beat.

ALAN. So sorry to hear about –

CATHERINE. Yes. Thank you.

ALAN. I wish you a long life.

CATHERINE. Well, there's no need for that. Feels quite long enough.

ALAN. It's just a saying. I don't really know why people say it. Especially during times of suffering. But then we like a bit of suffering – don't we? It's where we get our sense of humour from. (*Beat.*) Say something, Tom.

TOM. I got you a card.

ALAN. It's from both of us.

TOM. No, it's not.

ALAN. It's got a poem in it.

TOM. Alan doesn't want to do this any more.

ALAN. I'm sorry to let you down, Princess. But that David's a bad man.

TOM. His success is your success.

ALAN. He's a con. That man owes me.

CATHERINE. He owes me too.

TOM. And me. Well, I need to speak to him.

ALAN. We all need to speak to him.

Beat.

So what happens now?

CATHERINE. We wait for David.

They look at the platter of sandwiches.

Black.

End of Act One.

ACT TWO

On the screen large numbers appear in quick succession:
'49', '42', '35', '28', '21'…

(14)

…A large '14' appears on the TV screen. Then disappears.

Lights up. The TV is now a window on the city, circa 1973.

ALAN *stands.* TOM *and* CATHERINE *sit on the sofa in their usual formation. They are all 14.* TOM, *in addition, wears a school-uniform tie.* CATHERINE *has a school boater hat in her possession.* ALAN *is in a leather jacket and midway through singing 'Young Love' by Donny Osmond, loudly.*

He finishes. Silence. CATHERINE *and* TOM *stare at him blankly.*

CATHERINE. I prefer Suzi Quatro. Or Sylvia Plath.

ALAN. Is she in the charts?

CATHERINE. No.

    She smiles at TOM. TOM *smiles.*

ALAN. You wanna job, Tommy?

TOM. No, thank you.

ALAN. Lose your virginity in no time. Birds come flocking to my stall. Like flies round shit.

TOM. I'm going to university first.

ALAN. Why?

TOM. I want a *good* job.

ALAN. University of Life, me.

TOM. It's a means to an end, really. I'm waiting for my life to begin.

CATHERINE. I know what you mean.

TOM. Do you?

CATHERINE. God. Yes. I hate school.

ALAN. So what ya gonna do when your life begins then?

TOM. Make my own decisions.

ALAN. Like what?

TOM. I haven't decided yet.

CATHERINE. I think you should be a poet.

ALAN. A poet?

CATHERINE. You have an air of Ted Hughes about you.

ALAN. You know, people say I've got a bit of Donny Osmond in me. (*Sings*.) '*Young love…*'

TOM. More like *five* Donny Osmonds.

CATHERINE. The whole family.

CATHERINE *smiles at* TOM. *Discretely she lets her hand touch his, then holds it. Oblivious,* ALAN *continues to sing 'Young Love'.*

Black.

(49) – The Home Interviews

ALAN (*49*) *sits on a chair in his flat. He wears trousers and a shirt, no tie. His jacket hangs over the back of the chair. He looks out front as if talking to camera.*

ALAN. Are you rolling?

So this is it. The city pad. My 'pied-à-terre'. Don't get much for your money in East London. Not any more. Prices have gone – (*Whistles, indicates a rise and then a plateau with a hand gesture.*) They know how to maximise space, though. In the kitchenette they've done this very clever thing with the oven. There isn't one. Instead, there's a microwave that bakes and grills. Brilliant.

I suppose, *technically* this is more Bethnal Green than Shoreditch. Shoreditch *Borders*. When I was growing up, Shoreditch was a shithole. According to my daughter, Sophie, it's full of artists. You know, kids with bad haircuts. She had an exhibition. In a gallery. Just around the corner. She invited me. Normally she says I won't *get* it. There was a room that you went into with all these dead chicken car-casses suspended from the ceiling. Hundreds of 'em. With their guts all hanging out. And there was this smell being pumped in. It was called *Waste*. Now, call me a philistine, to me that's not art. That's a fucking abattoir.

Would you like another cup of tea? Beigel? They're locally sourced. Just about.

He takes a bite from a bagel.

No. This place is very handy. I stay here a lot during the week. And weekends. If I'm working. I think Toni can get a bit lonely, though. She lost her keys a few months ago. To the house. She went into a blind panic, changed all the locks. Even the windows. Do you know how much it is to call out a locksmith? *Ninety quid an hour*. They used to be the working class – tradesmen. Now they make more money than me. It's all change.

TOM (*49*) *is wearing the brightly patterned jumper. There's a half-empty glass of water by him.*

TOM. She wrote to me. She writes to people she sees on TV. Normally, I don't answer them. But she sent a photo with hers, and I thought she looked rather nice. See –

He takes a small photo out of his pocket and shows it 'to camera'.

Then one day she turned up at my work. The archive. She walked straight up to Customer Requests and said, 'I'm looking for Tom. Tell him Leesa's here, and he hasn't answered my letter.' I thought she might be a bit of a nutter. But she's very pretty in real life. And bubbly. And loud. We're quite different personalities. But I guess opposites do attract, because I asked her to marry me and she said 'yes'. Well, it was her idea. But as she said, I'm not getting any younger. We got married six months and fourteen days after we met. She really has turned my life around.

Married men have the lowest rate of clinical depression.

Happily married men. Divorced men have the highest. For women it's different.

One of the things Leesa's taught me is to talk about my feelings. There used to be a terrible stigma about clinical depression, but now it seems everyone's talking about it. When I was seven it was unheard of for a child to be depressed. By the time I had my breakdown at Cambridge it was too late. I couldn't even get out of bed. Couldn't wash. Couldn't think straight. It was the pressure mainly. The anxiety. The fear of failure.

Pause. He takes a swig of his water and then holds up the glass.

It's half-full.

It's a half-full glass of water.

It's taken me nearly forty-nine years to understand that.

CATHERINE (*49*) *sits on a sofa in her house. She wears a cardigan, blouse and skirt. She looks tired. Again, she talks to camera.*

CATHERINE. I was watching a tape of the interview with Martin Bashir. And I thought, she knows exactly what she's doing. It all seemed a bit... contrived. The head cocked to one side. Those eyes. Down. The overwhelming vulnerability. If it was an act, she was bloody good at it. She really pissed off the Queen. All those flowers. People travelled for miles. Just for her. Sometimes I see flowers tied to railings. You know, where someone's died in a car accident. I wonder what happened.

I picked up Geoffrey from the airport the other day. He tells me not to bother because of the parking. NCP charges a fortune. Normally he gets the train, but his flight was delayed and it was late. So I thought it would be nice. I still get a kick seeing him walk through arrivals. He got straight in the car and switched on the radio. He wanted to hear the news. But we went into a tunnel and the signal disappeared. Well, he looked so annoyed. Angry even. And I suddenly thought about driving into the wall. Turning sharply. Swerving to the left. The scraping of metal. The traction against the side of the car. The pull of the steering wheel. The dull thud of hitting the pillar head-on. And what must have been going through her mind. Dodi. Her sons. The log flume at Alton Towers. She took them there. It was an outing for her and the boys. She was wearing a brown leather jacket. Being a '*cool Mum*'. She wanted them to have a reality. Away from the eyes of the world. But then I remembered all the photographers. The press call. Her smile. That brown leather jacket.

Apparently, your entire life flashes before you.

I asked Thomas if he wanted to go to Alton Towers with me, and he laughed. 'Not cool, Mum,' he said. 'Not cool at all.'

You just want them to be happy, don't you? You want to know that if you weren't there, they'd be all right. They'd cope. And part of you, deep down, hopes that they wouldn't. They couldn't possibly survive without you. The world wouldn't be the same. You'd be universally mourned. And the flowers. There'd be thousands of flowers from total and utter strangers. There'd be famous people at your funeral you didn't even know. And David would do a eulogy. And there'd be a pop concert arranged in your honour. Christ, do you really think she wanted Donny Osmond there? She was an anarchist. She rocked the establishment. And then ten years later, a middle-aged Donny Osmond's singing 'Coat of Many Colours' at Wembley Stadium.

ALAN. Work's great. We're downsizing. Well, you have to move with the times, don't you? Nowadays everything fits into an iPod. The high street's practically dead. We're making a move into the virtual knicker market. Underwear online. We're trying to get a celebrity endorsement. It's all about celebrity now – putting a face to the knickers. Actually, I thought David might be able to help. He's doing bloody well, isn't he. *Annihilation* (*End of the World*): *Part Two*. How much did that gross then? Do you know if he's coming? I know you said he couldn't *today*, but he will be coming to the main interview, won't he? With all three of us. It would be nice to see him. Oh. Don't get me wrong. I still get recognised on the street. Hounded.

Doorbell rings.

Just ignore it. I'm on a roll here.

Doorbell rings.

Probably someone to read the meter.

Doorbell rings again.

Keep quiet for a minute. They'll go away.

Beat.

Where was I?

There's a banging on the door.

(*Shouts.*) Daniel, is that you?

TOM *is holding up a book.*

TOM. Leesa and I wrote a book. *The Twelve Steps of Marriage: From Depression to Happiness.* There's a foreword by Dr Raj Persaud. The first step is admittance. '*I am depressed.*' We do book tours and seminars. Sold out in Birmingham. Did you know, since I started talking, nearly two hundred people have realised they're depressed. Anyway… Leesa wanted me to show you.

He puts the book down.

There's a DVD. And a clothing range – we struck a deal with George at Asda. And of course, there's the film. I wrote a new one. I've had some interest from Hollywood. I'll be flying out there next month. Oh, it's been a very productive time. It's almost like you have to hit rock bottom before things get better.

ALAN *enters back into his room. He looks harassed, but tries to cover it up.*

ALAN. Well, it wasn't Daniel. Shame. He's got big now. Bigger than his old man. Scares the shit out of me.

He pops round quite a bit. For the telly. We watch the match together. Sometimes.

Oh, I know what you're thinking. Where is the TV? Well, this is a funny story. Daniel took it. Said he wanted to borrow it… hasn't brought it back. Little bugger. And my mobile phone. He said he'd get me an upgrade. Kids are so media-savvy nowadays.

Mind you, we didn't have the opportunities they've had. The food. The money. The orthodontistry. Toni says I spoilt them. What ya gonna do? Of course you spoil 'em. They're your kids.

Thing is about the phone... it had David's number on it. And I was just wondering if you could –

There's a knock at the door. ALAN *stops.*

Black.

(49)

A large '49' appears on the TV screen. Then disappears.

Lights up. The screen is again a window over the city, circa 2008.

All is as before, including the large silver platter of assorted sandwiches by the sofa.

TOM *(49) and* CATHERINE *(49) sit in their usual positions.* CATHERINE *is looking at the photo of Leesa.*

CATHERINE. What's her name?

TOM. Leesa. With two 'E's.

CATHERINE. She's very pretty.

TOM. Do you think so?

CATHERINE. How old is she?

TOM. Twenty-four. But you wouldn't know it.

CATHERINE. No.

TOM. She's had quite a full life. This is her second marriage.

CATHERINE. Well, I wish you lots of luck.

She hands back the picture.

TOM. She's a big fan of yours.

CATHERINE. Is she?

TOM. Yes. She'd really like to meet you.

CATHERINE. That's nice.

TOM. She's waiting in the Green Room.

CATHERINE. Couldn't find a babysitter?

TOM. She's here to stop me saying stupid things.

CATHERINE. Really.

TOM. She thinks David asks provocative questions.

Catherine, I wanted to say –

CATHERINE. How's the sex?

TOM. Pardon?

CATHERINE. Is it a midlife crisis?

TOM. I'm sorry?

CATHERINE. Why do you fancy women half your age? Those sort of questions.

TOM. Erm. Well… Yes. Sort of. She wanted to give you a copy of our book, *Twelve Steps of Marriage*. There's a chapter on grief –

CATHERINE. I've read it.

TOM. Have you?

CATHERINE. Yes.

TOM. Did it help?

CATHERINE. No.

TOM. What about 'thoughts for the day'?

CATHERINE. Trite.

TOM. Oh. Right. How's Geoffrey?

CATHERINE. Fine. We're both fine.

TOM. I read about it in the paper. At work.

CATHERINE. Which one?

TOM. Sorry?

CATHERINE. Which paper?

TOM. Erm… *The Mirror.*

CATHERINE (*she thinks*). '*Annus horribilis* for TV Princess.'

TOM. There was a photo. I nearly didn't recognise you, but
    they put the seven-year-old one next to it –

CATHERINE. I looked terrible.

TOM. I thought you looked lovely.

CATHERINE. The camera's so horribly unforgiving. I should
    do something. Get some make-up. I feel pale.

    *She rummages around in her bag, pulls out a mirror and
    looks at herself.*

TOM. Catherine –

CATHERINE. God. I look ghostly. I shouldn't have looked.

TOM. I wanted to get in touch –

CATHERINE. I look at my face in the mirror, I start finding
    things – things that don't belong to me. That line. In the
    corner of my eye. I've never seen that line before. Suddenly
    there's a line. And you cover it up, and it highlights some-
    thing else. The dark patch of skin underneath. So you cover
    that. And then something else. It's like a bloody avalanche.

    You look exactly the same, of course. You always do.

TOM. I don't.

CATHERINE. I hate the way men do that. No avalanche for
them.

TOM. Catherine –

CATHERINE. No shifting sand. No tectonic movement.

TOM. I really am sorry for your loss.

CATHERINE. It's only looks, Tom.

TOM. No. I mean –

CATHERINE. Age eventually happens to us all. Even Leesa
with two 'E's.

TOM. Are you sure you're okay?

CATHERINE. I don't want to dislike younger women. It's so…
unsisterly. But, fuck it, they just make me feel like a sack of
shit. Thank God I didn't have a daughter. It's so distasteful to
be jealous of one's children. Don't you think?

TOM. I don't know.

Beat.

Your *son*, Catherine… I'm so sorry.

CATHERINE. Thank you.

TOM. All the press intrusion. It must have been very hard.

CATHERINE. You just have to know how to play them.
Manipulating the press – it's like holding up a shield to
deflect a bullet. They've been very helpful with the MADD
campaign.

TOM. MADD?

CATHERINE. Mothers Against Drink Drivers.

TOM. Of course.

CATHERINE. I'm here to raise the campaign's profile.

TOM. I see.

CATHERINE. Where's Alan?

TOM. Talking to a production assistant.

CATHERINE. I hope he's not going to muck us about.

TOM. Catherine –

CATHERINE. He can't walk out today. He'll spoil everything.
Maybe I should have a word –

She goes to get up.

TOM. No, wait! Can't we talk for a bit?

CATHERINE. You want to talk.

TOM. I've been encouraged to. I've got a therapist.

CATHERINE. Good for you.

TOM. He's very expensive.

CATHERINE. I'm sure he's worth it.

TOM. He nods a lot. Makes this 'mmm' sound. Sometimes he
closes his eyes when I'm speaking. He pretends he's deep in
thought, when he's actually asleep. I think he finds me boring.

Catherine?

CATHERINE. Mmm?

TOM. I'm not sure if it's working. I still wake up very early.

CATHERINE. Would you like a sleeping pill? I've got some in
my purse.

TOM. You shouldn't take pills!

CATHERINE. They're not very strong.

TOM. Pills numb the senses. They don't fix the problem.

CATHERINE. What does fix it, Tom?

TOM. Have you tried cognitive behavioural –

CATHERINE. I've tried everything. Hypnotherapy.
Hydrotherapy. Craniosacral therapy. Counselling. Once
every three weeks Geoffrey and I are encouraged to talk
about our *differences*. Apparently it's very normal for
couples not to be in the same place with grief. Although
there is a school of thought it can bring couples closer
together. Tragedy, in some way, being a *uniting* element. As
seen with the survivors of 9/11. Or indeed with the contest-
ants on *Big Brother*. Is that in your book?

TOM *shakes his head*. CATHERINE *takes a lipstick from
her bag*.

He offered to get a job closer to home. But I like the dis-
tance, it suits me. Having the house to myself. I listen to The
Pistols on Geoffrey's Bose sound system. Whack it up until
the French windows vibrate. Pogo dance about. Scream.
Without any guilt. Because that's all part of it too, isn't it?
The blame. The recriminations.

TOM. You mustn't blame yourself.

CATHERINE. I don't blame myself… Not at all.

TOM. That's good.

CATHERINE. I blame this programme.

TOM. Sorry?

CATHERINE. I blame David.

TOM. Well, I don't know –

CATHERINE. Remember your rats, Tom? Point a camera at
them, and things start to happen. I think people in the public
eye actually attract tragedy. Look at them – the Windsors.
The Kennedys. Britney Spears…

TOM. It's not the same thing.

CATHERINE. Why do you think your car insurance is higher
than everyone else's?

TOM. I don't own a car.

CATHERINE. It's utter hubris to think we can flaunt our lives in front of the nation, and not have to pay the price.

TOM. It was an accident.

CATHERINE. It was premeditated murder. David offered us up like sacrificial lambs.

TOM. You mustn't do this to yourself –

CATHERINE. He said, 'Here they are… Three seven-year-old children. Come on, gods. Let's see what you can do.' So I ranted on about not wanting kids, and they take my bloody son –

TOM. He was hit by a drink driver.

CATHERINE. You read the papers – the crossing by the night-club. Blood alcohol levels. The amount of drugs my son had in his system. That he wasn't looking when he crossed the road. And the inquest that said no one was one hundred per cent to blame. Except of course that's not true.

TOM. It was a terrible accident.

CATHERINE. I'm suing David.

TOM. What?

CATHERINE. I'm issuing him with a writ during the interview.

TOM. You can't.

CATHERINE. Why not? Al Fayed sued the Royals.

TOM. He didn't win. He was a laughing stock.

CATHERINE. But he was right. It wasn't just an accident. Someone murdered his son.

TOM. David's not a murderer.

CATHERINE. David has steered the entire course of my life. Now I'm the one taking control.

TOM. They won't show it, Catherine. They won't put it on air.

CATHERINE. They will if it makes good TV. Let's face it, that's what this is all about.

He grabs hold of her.

TOM. Don't do it.

CATHERINE. Tom –

TOM. Please. Say you won't.

CATHERINE. Let go of me.

TOM. Think about David.

CATHERINE. I want his head on a plate.

TOM. Think about *Alan*. What it'll do to him.

CATHERINE. I've made up my mind –

TOM. You'll destroy him. This programme means everything to him.

ALAN *storms in. His face looks quite orange, apart from some very light patches under his eyes.*

ALAN. I'm not doing this. I've had enough.

TOM. Alan?

During the next speech ALAN *starts rummaging around under the cushions of the sofa.*

ALAN. They won't give me the tapes back. My interviews. Of *me*. There'd be no show without us. No fucking social experiment. Upper. Middle. Lower. And below that. Below the lowest of the working class are the people who work in TV. The scum. The cockroaches.

He sticks his hand under CATHERINE*'s cushion.*

'Scuse me, Princess.

CATHERINE. What are you doing?

ALAN. Checking for loose change. For the cab fare home. They won't get me a car.

CATHERINE. What's happened to your face?

ALAN. I got attacked by two make-up girls and a Touche Éclat.

ALAN stops and looks out front.

Is that camera on?

TOM. Alan –

ALAN. Are we being recorded?

TOM. Catherine said –

ALAN. What?

TOM. Erm –

CATHERINE. Would you like a sandwich?

ALAN. No. I'd like some answers. I'd like David to turn up, and treat us with some bloody respect. More control. More money. More – (*He stops.*)

What type of sandwiches?

CATHERINE. There's cucumber, ham and tomato, corned beef –

ALAN. Any egg mayonnaise?

TOM. No.

CATHERINE. Hang on. I'll have a dig around.

CATHERINE pokes around the sandwiches.

TOM. No. There isn't!

CATHERINE licks her fingers.

CATHERINE. He's right. That's cream cheese. Does anyone have a napkin?

TOM. No. Sorry.

CATHERINE. Alan, it will be very inconvenient if you pull out today. Dare I say – selfish. Do you have a napkin?

ALAN. It's sewn in.

CATHERINE. I've got something to give David.

TOM. No. She hasn't.

CATHERINE. Where is he?

ALAN. On his way.

    CATHERINE *goes to exit*. TOM *panics*.

TOM. Think about what you're doing.

CATHERINE. I'm washing my hands, Tom.

    He watches her go.

TOM. Please don't pull out, Alan.

ALAN. Nothing to do with you. It's between me and David.

TOM. You want money?

ALAN. I want what's owed to me.

TOM. You've used this programme to promote your business.

ALAN. Let me tell you something, sunshine. Right now the angel of retail death is passing over my shops. Killing them one by one. My first-born – on Commercial Road – an internet café. When David starts paying my bills, my tax, my mortgage, my wife's slate at the hairdresser's – which, I can assure you, would put Donald Trump in a sticky situation – then I'll owe him.

TOM. I'll give you the money, Alan.

ALAN. Don't be stupid.

TOM. How much?

ALAN. You haven't got that sort of cash.

TOM. I'll write you a cheque.

ALAN. It's unquantifiable. The aggravation, the loss of business –

TOM. Just say a figure.

ALAN. Fifty grand.

TOM. *Fifty?*

ALAN. More if you've got it.

TOM. I don't. Not straight away. I can get it for you.

ALAN. When?

TOM. As soon as they pay for the film.

ALAN. Christ.

TOM. I've done it, Alan. I've become a success.

ALAN. Tom... Tommy... Listen, mate. I hate to break it to you. You're not a success.

TOM. I am. I get my vegetables delivered. Organic.

ALAN. You're middle. You're average. You're not going anywhere. Your life is stuck in middle-class limbo.

TOM. I am going somewhere.

ALAN. You've had nothing to climb up. Nowhere to go. Nothing to struggle against.

TOM. I've struggled.

ALAN. Against what?

TOM. Myself.

ALAN. Big deal.

TOM. My environment. The pressure.

ALAN. Textbook middle-class angst. *Status anxiety*. It's in your book. Chapter Five.

TOM (*surprised*). You read my book?

ALAN. I got the audio tape.

In a bargain bucket at Heston Services.

TOM *stops smiling*.

Thing about depression, Tom – it's a middle-class disease. Working classes, we haven't got time for it. We're too busy struggling to make ends meet.

TOM. But I'm better now. I'm happy. I'm moving on.

ALAN. You, my friend, are staying right where you are.

TOM. I'm going to Hollywood.

ALAN. Hollywood?

TOM. Los Angeles.

America.

ALAN. Good for you. Piece of advice – don't bother with Disneyland. The one in Florida's better.

TOM. MGM Studios.

ALAN. Now, that is a good one. They do this Spaghetti Western reconstruction. And the Walk of Stars. You know, I have exactly the same size hands as Clint Eastwood.

TOM. They've bought the rights to my script.

ALAN. You what?

TOM. They're making my film.

ALAN. *Brief Encounter*?

TOM. No. They've already done that one.

ALAN. They're doing a remake?

TOM. No. My *new* film. About *me*. They're turning my life into a movie.

ALAN. Your life?

TOM. Yes.

ALAN. They're turning *your* life into a film?

TOM. Yes.

> ALAN *starts laughing*.

> What?

ALAN. Hollywood?

TOM. Yes.

ALAN. That's a good one.

TOM. It's true.

ALAN. Never Never Land.

TOM. I swear.

ALAN. On whose life – Billy Liar?

TOM. The contracts are ready. There's a director attached. But David's so desperate to do it. It's gone to a bidding war. As we speak.

> ALAN *stops laughing*.

ALAN. A bidding war?

TOM. Yes.

ALAN. Over you?

TOM. That's why he's late.

ALAN. Impossible.

TOM. Do you want to write yourself out of this, Alan? Because if you leave, that's what will happen.

ALAN. What?

TOM. You won't be in the story any more.

ALAN. You're bluffing.

TOM. I'm not.

ALAN. David wants to do it?

TOM. He feels very close to the material.

ALAN. Who's the other director?

TOM. Mel Gibson.

>   ALAN *starts laughing again.* TOM *is getting very frustrated.*

>   And he's going to be in it.

ALAN. He's gonna be in it?

TOM. As an actor.

ALAN. Who's he playing?

TOM. Me.

ALAN. Who's playing *me*?

TOM. Actually, he's got a bit of a problem with your part.

ALAN. I bet he has.

>   Who's playing Catherine?

TOM. Jodie Foster

ALAN. That's not right.

TOM. She's a very good actress.

ALAN. Not pretty enough.

TOM. She's won an Oscar.

ALAN. No. No. No. You need someone pretty. And English. And not a lesbian. (*Thinks.*) Have you seen that woman in the Green Room?

TOM. What woman?

ALAN. The blonde.

Beat.

Blonde girl. Lovely legs.

TOM. What about her?

ALAN. That's the sort of girl you're looking for. Maybe she's a bit young –

TOM. She's not an actress.

ALAN. Oh. All women are actresses. Just throw some money at 'em.

TOM. I don't think so.

ALAN. She's the spit of Catherine. I was watching her. And there must have been some magnetic force. Coz she turned her head and smiled at me.

TOM. Did she?

ALAN. Oh. Yeah. Beautiful set of teeth. Like a fucking angel –

TOM *jumps up and grabs* ALAN *by the collar.*

TOM. You leave her alone.

ALAN. Jesus, Tom.

TOM. You understand.

ALAN. What's up?

TOM. My smile. My angel. My wife.

ALAN. Your wife?

TOM. Yes.

ALAN. She's married to you?

TOM. *My wife!*

ALAN. All right.

TOM. So you leave her alone.

ALAN. I didn't touch her.

TOM. Keep your filthy smile away from her.

ALAN. She smiled at *me*.

TOM. You understand?

ALAN. Fine. Fine. Can you loosen your grip?

TOM. Not your property. Not your business. Not your struggle.

ALAN. Sorry.

TOM. Mine.

ALAN. I said I'm sorry.

TOM. I mean it.

ALAN. Okay.

> TOM *keeps his hold on* ALAN*'s shirt, but his body is no longer aggressive. He begins to wilt.*

> My shirt, Tom.

TOM. You don't understand.

ALAN. I understand. You're creasing it.

TOM. You've been married to Toni for how long?

ALAN. Erm… I can't –

TOM. It's a long time.

ALAN. I can't count without oxygen. Lack of oxygen, Tom.

TOM. Twenty-six years.

ALAN. Is it really?

TOM. You take marriage for granted.

ALAN. I don't.

TOM. You do.

TOM *tightens his grip*.

ALAN. I do. Yes. I do.

TOM. I've been alone, Alan. *Alone*.

ALAN. I know.

TOM. You don't know.

ALAN. Everyone knows.

TOM. You don't realise what that means until you've felt it.

ALAN. Yes. I mean, *no*. Look. Can you let go.

TOM. You have to do this programme, Alan. You and
    Catherine. If the show ends, Leesa will leave me.

ALAN. Really?

TOM. I'll be a failure. That's what she said.

ALAN. No.

TOM. She said it.

ALAN. She doesn't *mean* it. Wives always say things they
    don't mean.

TOM. Really?

ALAN. Yes. Like 'I do'. That's marriage. Good with the bad.
    Ups and downs. Swings and roundabouts.

TOM. I can't get divorced. Divorced men have the highest rate
    of depression.

ALAN. Tom. My shirt –

    TOM *stops and looks at* ALAN's *face. A beat.* TOM *looks
    closely – like he might kiss him*.

    What?

    TOM *studies his face*.

    What are you looking at?

TOM. What's wrong with your eyes?

ALAN. Nothing.

TOM. There's something –

ALAN. Where's Princess got to?

TOM. She's gone to wash her hands. There's definitely something wrong with your eyes.

ALAN. It's nothing.

TOM. Yes. You've got little crosses under your eyes. Both of them.

ALAN. No, I don't.

TOM. You do. I can see them.

ALAN. Let go of me. You're making the blood rush to my head. I've got blood pressure.

TOM. Have you – ?

   TOM *starts laughing. He lets go of* ALAN*'s shirt.* ALAN *straightens his collar.*

ALAN. What's so funny?

TOM. You have. Haven't you?

ALAN. That's it. Have a good laugh. You and the make-up girls. Go on.

TOM. You've had your bags removed.

ALAN. Yes. And it bloody hurts.

   TOM *laughs louder.*

   Thanks for the sympathy. I hope the wind changes and your face stays like that.

TOM. What – like this?

   TOM *pulls the skin down under his eyes and pulls a funny face.* CATHERINE *enters.*

CATHERINE. What's going on?

TOM. Alan's had plastic surgery.

ALAN. I can't do the programme like this. It looks like
    someone's been playing Noughts and Crosses on my face.

CATHERINE. There's a huge crowd of people outside the studio.

    TOM *and* ALAN *go to look out of the window.*

ALAN. Who are they?

CATHERINE. Fans.

ALAN. What are they holding?

CATHERINE. Placards. With our names on them.

TOM. My name?

CATHERINE. All of us. Oh. And Tom – your wife's out there
    trying to sell T-shirts. She's about to be arrested for illegal
    trading.

TOM. She promised she wouldn't.

    TOM *runs out.*

ALAN. You've seen Tom's wife.

CATHERINE. Yes.

ALAN. She's gorgeous.

CATHERINE. Yes.

ALAN. And young –

CATHERINE. I know.

ALAN. Not a patch on you.

CATHERINE. Thank you.

ALAN. Neither's Jodie Foster.

CATHERINE (*slightly confused*). Thank you.

CATHERINE sits down and opens her bag. She pulls out a make-up compact.

Would you like me to fix your make-up?

ALAN. Oh. No.

CATHERINE. You want people to see you like that?

She holds up the mirror to ALAN's face. ALAN looks at himself.

ALAN. Christ.

CATHERINE. I couldn't make it worse. Sit down.

ALAN nods, sits and holds his face up to her. She starts to apply powder to ALAN's face.

ALAN. My sister used to do this to me.

CATHERINE. How is your sister?

ALAN. We fell out.

CATHERINE. I thought you were close.

ALAN. She tried to sue me.

CATHERINE. What on earth for?

ALAN. Libel. She didn't like the way I talked about her on the programme.

CATHERINE. I'm sure you'll make it up.

Done!

CATHERINE starts applying make-up to herself – mascara, powder, lipstick. ALAN watches.

ALAN. How's Geoffrey?

CATHERINE. Fine.

How's Toni?

ALAN. Fine.

CATHERINE. The children?

ALAN. Oh. Great. Great. I saw Sophie the other day. Well, a few weeks ago now. We went out for lunch.

CATHERINE. Is she working in fashion?

ALAN. No. She works in a bar. I told her she could get a better job. She could do anything she wanted with her brains. She told me not to interfere.

CATHERINE. They'll do what they want. They're free spirits.

ALAN. Dunno about free. They cost a bloody fortune, kids.

CATHERINE *finishes applying some lipstick. Silence.*
ALAN *looks at her.*

You know… You really are beautiful.

CATHERINE. Uh-huh.

ALAN. You are.

CATHERINE. Are you going to do the programme, or are you wasting my time?

ALAN. Remember that argument we had about Siouxsie Sioux?

CATHERINE. No.

ALAN. You were gorgeous.

CATHERINE. I was young.

ALAN. Still are.

CATHERINE. Not any more.

ALAN. I think you get more beautiful every time I see you. If I wasn't married –

CATHERINE. Give it a rest, Alan.

ALAN. If I'd met you thirty years ago –

CATHERINE. You did. *Forty-two.*

ALAN. I'd be all over you like a rash.

CATHERINE *looks at him.*

CATHERINE. Come on then.

ALAN. What?

CATHERINE. Put your money where your mouth is.

ALAN. What do you mean?

CATHERINE. Give us a go.

ALAN. Here?

CATHERINE. Yes.

ALAN. Now?

CATHERINE. Right here. Right now.

ALAN. Really?

CATHERINE. Absolutely.

ALAN. Are you sure?

CATHERINE. Are you all mouth and no trousers?

ALAN. No. Right… Well…

ALAN *hesitates.*

CATHERINE. Alan, are you just going to stand there, or are you going to come over and fuck me?

ALAN. God. I love it when posh birds talk dirty.

He runs over and launches himself at her. They stumble onto the couch. Kissing. Groping. He pulls off her cardigan. CATHERINE *starts unbuttoning his shirt.*

I've been dreaming about this for forty-two years.

CATHERINE. Since you were *seven*?

ALAN. I was an early developer.

I slept in the same bed as my sister.

More fumbling. CATHERINE *looks out front. She stops.*

CATHERINE. Alan?

ALAN. Say that again.

CATHERINE. Stop a minute.

ALAN. What?

CATHERINE. Do you think that camera's on?

ALAN. God. I hope so.

They lunge at each other again. He pulls up her skirt.

CATHERINE. We'll have to be quick.

ALAN. That's fine.

CATHERINE. What if Tom comes back?

ALAN. Trust me. I'll be quick.

She goes to unbutton his trousers. She stops. He stops.

Just carry on for a bit. I'll get there.

They carry on. ALAN *looks down at his crotch, frustrated.*

Come on!

CATHERINE. What's happening?

ALAN. Nothing.

CATHERINE. What's wrong?

ALAN. This has never happened before.

CATHERINE. Is there something I can do?

ALAN. No.

CATHERINE. Is it me?

ALAN. No.

CATHERINE. Are you sure?

ALAN. Maybe it's the anaesthetic from the operation?

CATHERINE. I have to say, this isn't doing much for my self-confidence.

ALAN starts to cry.

Alan?

ALAN. I'm sorry.

CATHERINE. Alan, pull yourself together.

ALAN. Toni's left me. She kicked me out and changed the locks.

She's run off with Trevor – my bloody accountant. He's bald. And short. And an *accountant*. I've never cheated on her. *Ever*. In over twenty-five years. I wouldn't.

He starts to sob. CATHERINE *hands him a napkin.*

And my business is going down the toilet. I'm broke. I spent all my money on an eye job because I'm getting old. And vain. And I didn't want Toni getting her hands on my last bit of cash. She's already got the house. And my bank details. Oh. And a few weeks after I moved into the flat – someone painted a swastika on my front door. I come home and there's this huge black swastika. And then a letter under the door saying, 'Go back home.' All my life I've known this neighbourhood.

This is my home.

CATHERINE. Did you call the police?

ALAN. They didn't do anything. They said people in the spotlight open themselves up to a bit of bad press.

I tried to speak to Toni, but she's changed the number.

CATHERINE. At least you've got the kids.

ALAN. God. Yes. I'm sorry.

He goes to hand back the napkin.

CATHERINE. No. Keep it.

ALAN. Thanks.

He blows his nose loudly. Beat.

Listen… erm… Do you think we can have another go? I might be able to –

CATHERINE. I don't think so.

ALAN. Sure. No. Of course.

CATHERINE. Sorry.

ALAN. There you go.

TOM staggers in, carrying a very large cardboard box. He dumps it on the floor. ALAN buttons his shirt. CATHERINE puts her cardigan back on, and reapplies her lipstick.

TOM. The crowd have gone mad.

ALAN. What's in the box?

TOM. Nothing.

CATHERINE. Has David arrived?

TOM. Not yet.

ALAN goes over to the box. He puts his hand in.

Don't touch it. Alan!

ALAN pulls out a white T-shirt. He holds it up. The front is emblazoned with the slogan 'DON'T WORRY, BE HAPPY' in large letters. ALAN turns the T-shirt around. On the back is an image of TOM's face.

CATHERINE puts her hand in the box and pulls out another T-shirt. She opens it up. It bears the slogan – 'TOM SAYS RELAX'.

ALAN starts laughing.

ALAN. What the hell is this?

TOM. Put it back.

ALAN. This schmuttah.

TOM. Leesa designed them.

ALAN. Amazing workmanship.

TOM. Can you put it back, please.

ALAN. Let me have another look.

TOM. I mean it, Alan.

CATHERINE. I was thinking of releasing a single. For the MADD campaign.

ALAN (*reading the label on the T-shirt*) 'Made in China.'

TOM *launches himself at* ALAN *and grabs hold of the T-shirt.* ALAN *doesn't let go.*

What are you doing?

TOM. Give it to me.

ALAN. I'm only having a look.

CATHERINE. A *cover* obviously. Everything's a cover of something nowadays.

ALAN. You're gonna rip it.

TOM. Let go.

ALAN. *Relax.* You'll hurt yourself.

TOM. I'll hurt you.

ALAN. Are you threatening me?

TOM. You're a big, fat bully.

ALAN. What did you call me?

TOM. Nothing.

CATHERINE. Might even sing on it. Do a duet with that rock band Thomas was a fan of.

ALAN. Go on. Say what you just said.

TOM. I said, *let go*!

    TOM *pulls the T-shirt away.* ALAN*'s suit rips at the armpit.*

ALAN. Fucking hell. Look what you've done.

TOM. I'm sorry.

ALAN. That's bloody Armani.

TOM. I told you to let go.

ALAN. I can't do the programme in this.

TOM. You said you weren't doing it anyway.

ALAN. You little shit. Look at it.

CATHERINE. After all, we were the originals. The Arctic Monkeys can kiss my arse.

TOM (*to* ALAN). Are you doing the programme?

ALAN. Apologise.

TOM. No.

ALAN. Apologise for ripping my Armani.

TOM. I'm telling David on you.

ALAN. Do it.

TOM. You're a bully and a liar, Alan.

ALAN. You're paying for this suit.

TOM. That suit isn't Armani.

ALAN. Yes. It bloody is.

TOM. *Armani* only has one 'M', you illiterate oaf.

    ALAN *goes to grab* TOM. TOM *grabs his arm. The sleeve rips – a bit more than before.*

ALAN. Shit. Shit. Wait until I see David.

TOM. You started it.

ALAN. You ripped my suit.

TOM. He started it. Didn't he, Catherine?

> CATHERINE *suddenly jumps up and sings/screams a full-on, punk version of 'God Save the Queen', by The Sex Pistols. Shouting, head-banging, clothes-ripping, et al.*

> TOM *and* ALAN *stare at her.*

ALAN. Are you all right?

CATHERINE. I'm fine.

> *She goes to her bag and takes out an envelope. She goes to exit.*

TOM. Where are you going?

CATHERINE. To find David.

TOM. Will you come back?

> *She is gone.*

ALAN. What was that about?

TOM. Alan, are you doing the programme or not?

> ALAN *tries to straighten up his suit, and then attempts to read the label on the inside of his jacket.*

ALAN. Two 'M's.

TOM. Or are you just doing this to – (*He stops.*)

> What's that in your pocket?

> ALAN *quickly closes his jacket.*

ALAN. Nothing.

TOM. Open your jacket.

ALAN. No.

> TOM *tries to prise open* ALAN's *jacket.*

TOM. Show me.

ALAN. Get off!

> TOM *suddenly sticks his hand in* ALAN*'s inside pocket. Beat. He pulls his hand out – there's something on it.* TOM *raises his hand to his nose and sniffs it.*

TOM. Egg mayonnaise!

ALAN. What?

TOM. You've got an egg-mayonnaise sandwich in your pocket.

ALAN. No, I haven't.

TOM. Yes, you have.

ALAN. I haven't!

> TOM *tries to dive back into the pocket. A struggle.*

Let go!

> TOM *pulls out an egg-mayonnaise sandwich.*

TOM. Alan, what the hell are you doing?

ALAN. I thought I might be hungry later.

TOM. There's a whole tray of sandwiches here.

ALAN. I like egg mayonnaise.

TOM. Have you eaten them all?

> ALAN *doesn't answer.*

Alan, have you ever thought to consider that someone else might want an egg-mayonnaise sandwich?

ALAN. So have it!

TOM. I don't want it. It's been in your pocket.

ALAN. If you were starving, you'd eat it.

TOM. I want a fresh one!

ALAN. Then you should have been quicker.

TOM. Some fatty lardarse got there first!

> ALAN *grabs hold of* TOM*'s hand holding the sandwich, and tries to shove it into* TOM*'s mouth. Struggle.*

ALAN. Eat it!

TOM. No.

ALAN. Eat it.

TOM. Get off me – you greedy, overweight pig!

ALAN. You anaemic, little shit!

> ALAN *is just about to stuff the sandwich into* TOM*'s mouth, when he suddenly stops.*

TOM. Alan –

ALAN. Shush.

TOM. Let go of me.

ALAN. Shush.

TOM. What are you – ?

> ALAN *indicates the noise of a crowd outside, whistling and cheering.* ALAN *lets go of* TOM *and they move towards the window. They look out.*

What's she doing?

ALAN. Bloody hell.

TOM. Isn't it a bit cold to be doing that?

ALAN. By the looks of things – yes.

> TOM *moves even closer to the window. They're both transfixed. Beat.*

She's not a 34D any more.

TOM. Alan!

ALAN. It's my job.

TOM. Look. The police are chasing her.

More cheers from outside.

ALAN. She really is beautiful.

TOM. Yes. She is.

ALAN. Beautiful.

ALAN *adjusts his pants. He looks down.*

Oh. Now! *Now* you decide to work. Now you're awake.

TOM. I think she's going to bow out.

ALAN. She better not bow anywhere. I don't think I can take it.

ALAN *staggers over to the stage-right side of the sofa and sits.* TOM, *looking slightly bewildered, sits down next to him. Beat.*

TOM. Why don't you like me, Alan?

ALAN. What?

TOM. Have I done something to upset you?

ALAN. What you talking about?

TOM. You always give me such a hard time.

ALAN. You ripped my suit.

TOM. Not just today. Every time I see you.

ALAN. I'm just having a laugh.

TOM. Do I do something that annoys you?

ALAN. Not especially.

TOM. I must do something that gets on your nerves.

ALAN. Not really.

TOM. I'd like to know –

ALAN. It's nothing.

TOM. I think I wind you up.

ALAN. Okay. Yes. You do. You do wind me up, Tom. All right?

TOM. Do you want to talk about it?

ALAN. No.

TOM. My therapist says it's good to talk. Your mum used to say that.

ALAN. Don't talk about my mum.

TOM. I'm just saying. You shouldn't keep it all in –

ALAN. You've got no idea about my upbringing.

TOM. I've got a fair idea –

ALAN. All that middle-class comfort you were born into. You took it for granted. You fought it. You rejected it. You didn't have a clue how lucky you were. I would have loved half the opportunities you had. An education. A father. A dentist.

I've got crummy teeth.

TOM. I didn't feel very lucky.

ALAN. But you were, Tom. You *were*. You just think about it all too much.

TOM. I'm a success now. I've turned it around. I'm going to show people I've turned my life around.

ALAN. But they wanna see you fail. Don't you see, no one likes a success. They'll follow you on the up, and secretly hate you. Then they'll watch you come crashing down, and love you for it.

TOM. *Schadenfreude*.

ALAN. Sorry?

TOM. 'Taking delight in other people's misfortunes.' It's German.

ALAN. It would be.

TOM. So what do we do?

ALAN. I dunno.

Pause. TOM *offers him the platter of sandwiches.*

No. Cheers.

TOM *picks out a sandwich and eats it. They sit. After a moment,* ALAN *opens up his jacket and puts his hand into his inside pocket. He pulls out a sandwich and eats.*

TOM. Do you ever look back at the programmes, Alan?

ALAN *shrugs.*

ALAN. I dunno. Sometimes. You?

TOM. Sometimes. Leesa made me get a big TV. She said our kids'll grow up weird if we don't have one.

ALAN. You want them to have everything you didn't.

Is your wife expecting?

TOM. Not yet. She keeps feeding me pumpkin seeds. They're very good for male fertility.

ALAN. I didn't know that.

TOM. What if they end up like me?

ALAN. Your kids? Of course they'll be like you.

TOM. Exactly. No matter how positive and happy, and effervescent Leesa is. There's always going to be a possibility, a large probability, that they'll end up like me.

ALAN. But you're happy now, aren't you?

CATHERINE *enters. Her hair's a mess. Make-up smudged. She's breathless. She wears nothing except for an extra-large T-shirt with a picture of a giant butterfly on the front. On the back of the T-shirt – a giant Grecian urn. She looks at* TOM *and* ALAN.

CATHERINE. Do you remember when you were seven?

ALAN. You all right, Princess?

CATHERINE. I remember twenty-one… And fourteen… I'm struggling with seven.

ALAN. You had a hat. A straw one.

CATHERINE. Did I?

ALAN. Yeah. You were the bee's knees.

CATHERINE. Really?

ALAN. She was the bee's knees, wasn't she?

TOM. Erm –

CATHERINE. I'm forgetting everything.

ALAN. You remember – *seven*. Tom nearly wet himself.

TOM. No. I didn't.

ALAN. You did.

CATHERINE. Not just seven… twenty-eight… thirty-five…

TOM. The human brain's designed to forget. It's the only way we can survive.

CATHERINE. But I don't want to forget things. My life is relevant. Our *lives* are relevant.

ALAN. That's why we need the tapes.

TOM. I never wet myself.

ALAN. 'Nearly' wet yourself.

TOM. I'll ask David.

CATHERINE. We have to try and remember.

ALAN. We'll have a word with David.

TOM. David'll remember.

CATHERINE. David's not coming.

Beat.

ALAN. What?

TOM. Yes. He is.

CATHERINE. The second AD just told me.

ALAN. When?

CATHERINE. Just before.

ALAN. But they said –

TOM. He's on his way.

CATHERINE. He's still in Hollywood. He's making
    Annihilation (*End of the World*): *Part 3*.

ALAN. Part 3?

TOM. What about my film?

ALAN. What about my money?

TOM. He wants to make *my* film.

CATHERINE. He can't. He's too busy.

TOM. He promised me –

CATHERINE. He said we'd understand.

ALAN. He can't not come.

TOM. He can't do this to me. He promised me. I don't
    understand.

ALAN. We're his kids.

CATHERINE. Kids always blame their parents.

    TOM *presents the beginnings of an anxiety attack.*

TOM. David chose me. He told me I was special.

ALAN. He said that to all of us.

TOM. I wanted to be milk monitor. I never asked for this!

TOM starts to hyperventilate. He buries his head in the sofa, and starts to scream.

ALAN. What's he doing?

CATHERINE. He's having a tantrum.

He's overtired.

TOM throws the pillows off the sofa.

TOM. I'm not!

ALAN. I'm buggered. I'm dead. The sharks are gonna get me.

CATHERINE. Aaaaaah!

CATHERINE suddenly starts to scream and stomp around like a tantrum-ed toddler. She throws herself into the sofa. ALAN watches them.

ALAN. You're both nuts.

CATHERINE. It's therapeutic.

ALAN. You'll do yourselves an injury.

CATHERINE. Come on, Alan. Join in.

ALAN. My knee!

TOM. Regressive therapy.

CATHERINE. One… Two…

TOM. Three!

CATHERINE. Three!

ALAN. Jesus!

ALAN gives in and throws himself at the sofa. The sofa turns over. CATHERINE screams with delight. She picks up the tray of sandwiches and throws them at TOM and ALAN. Mayhem. It's a bunfight. TOM ducks for cover behind the sofa. CATHERINE *and* ALAN *grab a stash of sandwiches and ambush him.*

TOM (*shouting*). Stop! Stop!

He waves a white piece of paper from behind the sofa like a surrender flag.

ALAN. What is it?

CATHERINE. Are you all right?

ALAN. I told you somebody'd get hurt.

TOM *stands up. He holds up the paper.*

TOM. It's page thirty-five! *Ephemeral Moments.* (*He reads.*) 'He runs onto the platform as the guard's whistle sounds. She's boarding the train. He shouts to her...'

He drops the paper.

I love you.

ALAN. What?

TOM. I love you, Catherine. You are the bee's knees.

CATHERINE. Tom –

TOM. I do. I've always loved you.

ALAN. Are you mad?

TOM. No. Maybe. It depends who you talk to.

ALAN. You're married.

TOM. Yes.

ALAN. To Leesa.

TOM. Yes.

ALAN. She's next door.

TOM. I know this isn't a good time –

I've missed it, haven't I? I missed the train.

CATHERINE *smiles and touches* TOM*'s face.*

ALAN. What the hell's that?

He points to CATHERINE*'s tattoo.*

CATHERINE. My son. 'Tom.' He'll always be with me. We'll all get older and older, he'll always be twenty-one. In his second year of university. Forever young.

TOM. Like the Grecian urn.

CATHERINE. It was just an accident.

TOM. Yes.

CATHERINE. Accidents happen.

Beat.

ALAN. So what do we do now?

CATHERINE. We let it go.

ALAN. I can't let it go. They know who I am. They know where I live. I might as well kill myself now. They'd probably love that – watching me die on national television.

CATHERINE. So start again.

ALAN. I don't think I can.

CATHERINE. You're a survivor.

ALAN. I'm insolvent.

TOM. What am I going to do with all these T-shirts?

Beat.

What am I going to do with all these T-shirts, Alan?

A moment's silence.

ALAN. Here. What's a Grecian urn?

TOM. We've heard it.

ALAN. All right. Jesus.

Black.

(7)

A large '7' appears on the screen. Then disappears.

Lights up. The TV screen is again a large window offering a panoramic view of the city, circa 1966. The scene is restored. The sofa back in place. The sandwiches gone.

ALAN, TOM *and* CATHERINE *sit on the sofa (all aged 7). They all wear elements of school uniforms, all rather obviously from different schools.* ALAN *looks much more untidy than* TOM. CATHERINE *is in a straw hat.* TOM *needs the toilet.*

DAVID *is never seen. We hear his voice, like an old recording.*

DAVID. What does your father do?

CATHERINE *kisses* TOM *on the cheek.*

Catherine?

CATHERINE. He has a secretary. Mummy doesn't like to talk about it.

DAVID. Tom?

TOM. My father's a teacher.

ALAN *slaps him round the head.*

Ouch! David!

DAVID. Alan.

ALAN. I didn't touch him.

Beat.

DAVID. Can you answer the question?

ALAN. What?

DAVID. What does your father do?

ALAN. I don't know what he does. I dunno him.

DAVID. What do you want to be when you grow up?

CATHERINE *lifts up her skirt and flashes her knickers at* TOM.

ALAN. That's easy. I wanna be Steve McQueen. He's rich.

CATHERINE. I want to be a princess.

ALAN. You can't be a princess.

CATHERINE. Yes. I can. I'm going to marry Prince Charles.

ALAN. Show us your knickers.

DAVID. Tom?

TOM *looks at him.*

Look to camera.

TOM *looks out front.*

TOM. My parents want me to go to Oxbridge.

DAVID. Okay. But what do *you* want to do?

TOM. I want to go to the toilet.

DAVID. Alan, what would you do if you had a lot of money?

ALAN. I'd get a big house. With a big bath. And huge taps. And an indoor toilet.

TOM *crosses his legs and puts his hand up.*

DAVID. You don't need to put your hand up.

TOM. Can I go to the toilet, David?

CATHERINE. It's 'May I'.

TOM *looks out front. He looks desperate.*

TOM. May I?

Please.

Black.

The 'iconic' black-and-white picture of ALAN, TOM *and* CATHERINE *(at 7) appears on the screen. The screen flickers off.*

The End.

Stella Feehily
DUCK
O GO MY MAN

Debbie Tucker Green
BORN BAD
DIRTY BUTTERFLY
RANDOM
STONING MARY
TRADE & GENERATIONS

Ayub Khan-Din
EAST IS EAST
LAST DANCE AT DUM DUM
NOTES ON FALLING LEAVES
RAFTA, RAFTA...

Tony Kushner
ANGELS IN AMERICA – PARTS ONE & TWO
CAROLINE, OR CHANGE
HOMEBODY/KABUL

Elizabeth Kuti
THE SIX-DAYS WORLD
THE SUGAR WIFE

Liz Lochhead
EDUCATING AGNES ('The School for Wives') *after* Molière
GOOD THINGS
MEDEA *after* Euripides
MISERYGUTS & TARTUFFE *after* Molière
PERFECT DAYS
THEBANS

Linda McLean
ONE GOOD BEATING
RIDDANCE
SHIMMER
STRANGERS, BABIES

Conor McPherson
DUBLIN CAROL
McPHERSON: FOUR PLAYS
McPHERSON PLAYS: TWO
PORT AUTHORITY
THE SEAFARER
SHINING CITY
THE WEIR

Joanna Murray-Smith
BOMBSHELLS
THE FEMALE OF THE SPECIES
HONOUR

Bruce Norris
THE PAIN AND THE ITCH

Nina Raine
RABBIT

Ali Taylor
COTTON WOOL
OVERSPILL

Enda Walsh
BEDBOUND & MISTERMAN
DELIRIUM
DISCO PIGS & SUCKING DUBLIN
THE NEW ELECTRIC BALLROOM
THE SMALL THINGS
THE WALWORTH FARCE

Steve Waters
FAST LABOUR
THE UNTHINKABLE
WORLD MUSIC